Under Pressure

Diamond Mining and Everyday Life in Northern Canada

LINDSAY A. BELL

TC▶ TEACHING CULTURE
Ethnographies for the Classroom

UNIVERSITY OF TORONTO PRESS
Toronto Buffalo London

© University of Toronto Press 2023
Toronto Buffalo London
utorontopress.com

ISBN 978-1-4875-4827-8 (cloth)   ISBN 978-1-4875-4887-2 (EPUB)
ISBN 978-1-4875-4821-6 (paper)   ISBN 978-1-4875-4857-5 (PDF)

Library and Archives Canada Cataloguing in Publication

Title: Under pressure : diamond mining and everyday life in Northern Canada / Lindsay A. Bell.
Names: Bell, Lindsay A. (Anthropologist), author.
Series: Teaching culture.
Description: Series statement: Teaching culture : ethnographies for the classroom | Includes bibliographical references and index.
Identifiers: Canadiana (print) 20230150705 | Canadiana (ebook) 20230150772 | ISBN 9781487548216 (paper) | ISBN 9781487548278 (cloth) | ISBN 9781487548872 (EPUB) | ISBN 9781487548575 (PDF)
Subjects: LCSH: Diamond mines and mining – Canada, Northern. | LCSH: Diamond mines and mining – Social aspects – Northwest Territories – Hay River. | LCSH: Diamond mines and mining – Economic aspects – Northwest Territories – Hay River. | LCSH: Indigenous peoples – Northwest Territories – Hay River. | LCSH: Ethnology – Northwest Territories – Hay River. | LCSH: Hay River (N.W.T.) – Social conditions. | LCSH: Hay River (N.W.T.) – Economic conditions.
Classification: LCC TN994.C3 B45 2023 | DDC 338.4/7622382097193 – dc23

We welcome comments and suggestions regarding any aspect of our publications – please feel free to contact us at news@utorontopress.com or visit us at utorontopress.com.

Every effort has been made to contact copyright holders; in the event of an error or omission, please notify the publisher.

We wish to acknowledge the land on which the University of Toronto Press operates. This land is the traditional territory of the Wendat, the Anishnaabeg, the Haudenosaunee, the Métis, and the Mississaugas of the Credit First Nation.

University of Toronto Press acknowledges the financial support of the Government of Canada and the Ontario Arts Council, an agency of the Government of Ontario, for its publishing activities.

ONTARIO ARTS COUNCIL
CONSEIL DES ARTS DE L'ONTARIO
an Ontario government agency
un organisme du gouvernement de l'Ontario

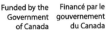

Funded by the   Financé par le
Government   gouvernement   Canada
of Canada   du Canada

Contents

Illustrations

Maps

Acknowledgements

When a book takes over a decade to complete, you amass a long list of debts of gratitude. Looking over the list of people in these acknowledgements is a reminder that it has been time well spent. First and foremost, I am thankful for the people who shared their knowledge with me and made this book possible. Thank you for your openness in providing a glimpse into your world so that we may all better understand ours.

So many Northern friends provided the support and insight that were essential to the research: Connie Belanger, Trisha Rhymes, Lisa Ruggles, Sophie Call, Ken and Vicky Latour, Kevin Wallington, and Patrick Poisson. Merci aux étudiants et enseignants à l'École Boréale qui m'accueille chaque fois que j'arrive dans le Nord. Ginger Gibson and Stephanie Irlbacher-Fox helped me to find my professional bearings at the start of my process.

The research for this book began in my doctoral program at the Ontario Institute for Studies in Education (OISE) University of Toronto. My supervisor, Monica Heller, is to thank for many of the skills needed to research like a grown-up. She was a generous mentor who set up the conditions in which her students could thrive. Mireille McLaughlin and Emmanuel DeSilva were my officemates and best interlocutors for sorting through ideas in those initial stages of study. My intellectual and political growth came from provocations from committee members Elizabeth Povinelli and Bonnie McElhinny. What a privilege it was to have your thoughts on my work. The Anthropology Department at the University of Toronto took me in as an intellectual refugee and for that I am forever grateful. Cohort mates Chantal Falconer, Aaron Kappeler, Sharon Kelly, Zoe Wool, Laura Sikstrom, Jessica Taylor, Kori Allan, and Olga Federenko made things lighter through shared struggles.

I was fortunate to have three resident fellowships that supported this work. First was a summer fellowship at the School for Advanced Research in Santa Fe, where it felt as if my cohort had been hand-picked for me to have the most engaging conversations. Hannah Voorhees, Gretchen Purser, and Mindy Morgan made that summer a highlight of this academic life. Next, Blue Mountain Centre offered me sustained time to work alongside Genevieve Scott, long-time friend and writer par excellence. She has been my go-to for advice and solidarity for well over ten years. If only we were neighbours all the time! Finally, Sari Pietikäinen invited me to be a "Language in a Changing Society" research fellow at the University of Jyväskylä, Finland, in 2016 and has been an incredible mentor ever since. She has read many drafts and heard long laments about this book. I am so very grateful. Kiitos!

There is a handful of scholars who love talking Northern stuff as much as I do. I am lucky to have Joshua Moses, Julia Christiensen, and Sara Komarnisky as both friends and colleagues. Kirk Dombrowski's book on culture politics in Alaska allowed me to do the kind of thinking I was longing for. He also taught me the value of "taking the crayons away."

Andrew Walsh, Elizabeth Ferry, and Annabel Vallard kindly invited me to participate in a Wenner-Gren workshop on the anthropology of precious minerals. There I met Filipe Calvao and Brian Brazeal, who taught me a lot about the workings of gem mining in other parts of the world.

I recruited professional help when I needed it most. Anne Amienne, writing coach and skills builder, you are to thank for turning my career around. I wish I had only known sooner that support was possible. Struggling writers reading this need to know that it is okay to ask for help. I had to learn that others were getting support by simply being more privileged.

I presented this material at Johns Hopkins University, Hamilton College, and Harvard University, where thought-provoking conversations with faculty and students changed the course of the book for the better. Tom Ozden Schilling, your kindness and commitment to my work feels undeserved. Bonnie Urciuoli and Chaise LaDousa provided an intellectual home away from home while in upstate New York.

Sandra Rosenthal provided compassion and support on every front. She invited me to participate in a writing group that got this book across the finish line. The generosity of Risa Cromer, Ken MacLeish, Carlota MacAllister, and Emily Yates-Doerr cannot be understated. Their own writing modelled so much of what I think is good in anthropology. Greg Beckett generously ran an online writing support group that helped troubleshoot any sticky points in the process. Thank you to the supportive members who provided insight and motivation to finish.

Thank you to the eager undergraduate assistants I've had over the years: Beth Coley, Victoria Ostrovsky, and Howard Boutelle. It has been fun to watch you soar. The talented Zoe Barriault led a student focus group so that I could get feedback from my target audience. The astute reading by Jessie Howard, Vanessa Ritsema, Alexandra Cini, Celine Tsang, and Josephine Bywaters showed me that sticking to the story is always the best plan. Madelyn Hertz, a talented PhD student, worked with me in the final hours of editing.

The art for the book, including the cover, came from my collaboration with Jesse Colin Jackson. In a strange instance of stars aligning, I found the one artist researcher who liked to talk about postwar towers as much as I do. Thank you for the parallel play that continues to be generative in how I think about the politics of representation and academic currency exchange.

Alana Ossa was a wonderful colleague at Oswego State who kept my spirits up. I have the pleasure of now calling Western's Anthropology Department home. My colleagues' kindness and support have meant the world to me. Kim Clark, Karen Pennesi, Dan Jorgensen, and Lisa Hodgetts are owed special thanks for their guidance. Ed Eastaugh made the maps for this book after a casual mention that I was in need.

Several friendships were particularly central to this work. Denielle Eliott is an inspiring anthropologist and comrade who makes me feel freer to write honestly. Khadija Coxon has heard about this work for way too long and taught me the value of organized thoughts and being straightforward. Tessa Murphy and Dipankar Rai kept me afloat during two maternity leaves and a pandemic. There are not enough ways to thank you both for the warmth you extend to me and my family. The GBC girls, you know what you mean to me.

My family has supported me in more ways than I can count. My mother did a lot of laundry in the hopes that this book might actually be done at one point. My siblings, Adam and Ashton, baba Luba, my dad, and Claire were all eager to see this come to fruition. Thank you!

Selections from chapter 3 ("Race") were initially published in the edited 2012 collection *21st Century Migration: Ethnography and Political Economy*, edited by Winnie Lem and Pauline Gardiner-Barber (Bell 2012). I am extremely grateful to both editors for their feedback on the many iterations of this piece. Some of the material in chapter 6 ("Morality") appears in my article "Soft Skills, Hard Rocks: Making Diamonds Ethical in Canada's Northwest Territories," published in 2017 in *Focaal: Journal of Global and Historical Anthropology*. Again, the reviewers and editors helped improve this piece and are owed thanks.

A conversation with Anne Brackenbury many years ago stayed with me and pulled me back to working with University of Toronto Press. By that time, she had moved on to bigger and better things, but her vision for this series guided me nonetheless. Carli Hansen received my manuscript warmly and helped sharpen it substantially. She gave me the deadlines I needed. No pressure, no diamond. Thank you to the anonymous reviewers for their comments. I could have done without Reviewer Two's tone, but I will say their close reading did the most to improve the work.

To my husband, David, and our children, Harrison Abijah and Stephanie Ulla, thank you for being my reason for wrapping this up so that we can spend more time together. I love you so much. You are my sacred and mundane.

CHAPTER ONE

Diamonds with a Story

The Smithsonian Museum of Natural History in Washington, DC, hosted Foxfire, a 187.7-carat uncut diamond, as a temporary guest in its gem collection in November 2016. Foxfire is the largest rough diamond mined in North America. It came from the Diavik diamond mine, one of three mines operating in the Northwest Territories in Canada, just north of the sixtieth parallel. Foxfire is the size of a small lime; however, size alone is not what makes it so valuable. In their press releases, both the museum and the mining corporation (Rio Tinto) stressed that the Foxfire diamond should be admired for its "fascinating provenance and ethical pedigree" (Amadena Investments 2017; Landers 2016).

The term "provenance" has two meanings. It can refer to place of origin and/or describe a record of ownership. In the case of Foxfire, these two meanings are inseparable. Geologists say the stone formed under pressure between 1 and 3 billion years ago and travelled from deep in the Earth's core via volcanic eruptions to settle into the bottom of what became lakes. In their marketing materials, Rio Tinto describes the northern region where the mines are as "pristine yet harsh" (Diamonds with a Story, n.d.). The unique landscape of the subarctic is a critical component of what sets Foxfire apart from other diamonds. Being from Canada is also integral to the notion of "ethical pedigree." Marketing materials stress that the diamond mines in Canada were "created in consultation with [I]ndigenous groups, which account for many of the mine's active staff" (Diamonds with a Story, n.d.). Northern diamonds were supposedly from a "pure" part of the world, both morally and environmentally.

I travelled to Washington to see Foxfire for myself. Although my life and research had been bound up with Northern diamonds for over a decade, I had yet to see one uncut. I hurried past replicas of large animals and dinosaur bones to the Janet Annenberg Hooker Hall of Geology, Gems, and Minerals on the second floor. At 20,000 square feet, it is one of the largest gem exhibition spaces in the world. The hall was crowded, and the flow of foot traffic was chaotic. People pinged back and forth between well-lit display cases. Stories of the history and material specificities of tiaras, pendants, and other luxury jewellery accompanied the most elaborate pieces. Diamonds make for good stories. Most famously, the Hope Diamond, a 45.52-carat diamond mined in the seventeenth century in India now set in a stunning pendant, is said to be cursed, bringing ill fortune to its owners. Now in the museum's permanent collection, the Hope Diamond and its stories draw the largest crowds. I waited in a jumbled line of patrons for ten minutes just to catch a glimpse.

Stories about minerals matter. In her book, *Clarity, Cut, and Culture: The Many Meanings of Diamonds* (2014, 2), anthropologist Susan Falls writes, "Our stories about diamonds not only reveal what we do with these tiny stones, but also suggest how we create value, meaning, and identity through our interactions with material culture in general." I have been intrigued by the storied life of diamonds since 2003, when I first moved to the Northwest Territories to work as an elementary school teacher. Living in a small Indigenous village in the high Arctic, I was far from the mines themselves but nevertheless would hear about them from local people debating the merits and risks of such a large-scale project. In my second year, I was transferred to a multi-ethnic community much closer to the mines. There, the optimism that mines would bring economic prosperity to the region was palpable. When I returned four years later as an anthropologist in training, I wanted to see how the promises of diamond-driven development were playing out. I was interested in following the lives of those trying to take up industry's promises for a secure future through work in mining. How were industry's claims to working with Indigenous communities being experienced by ordinary men and women in the region?

A central component of Foxfire's story at the Smithsonian was the opportunity for work and economic development for Indigenous people. As one of the world's richest mineral regions, prospective resource projects are often couched in terms of possibilities for local economic growth. Most of the public diamond stories I heard in northern Canada and across the country focused on economic opportunities like work and business development. On a preliminary trip to the territorial capital of Yellowknife in 2007 to finalize my fieldwork, I was taking stock of the vocational training opportunities linked to the expanding diamond industry. The modest city (population 19,000) was plastered with diamond imagery at every turn. Flags from lampposts declared the city "the diamond capital of North America!" At the visitors' centre, the historical timeline of the region began with a large 3D topographic map whose caption was "3 Billion Years in the Making," referring to the volcanic rock which ultimately becomes diamonds over time under the right conditions. A mosaic of portrait photographs of smiling local people, both Indigenous and not, lined a nearby wall. Each included a caption of how the diamond economy had improved their lives either through direct work in industry or in related sectors.

That year, Canada was the third-largest producer of rough diamonds in the world. Between my first arrival in 2003 and my return in 2007, the region's gross domestic product doubled largely due to the three open-pit mines operating well outside of town. Workers were flown into the mine sites for two-week shifts and then returned to their home communities for two weeks "out." In national and international news, the Northwest Territories (NWT) was becoming the site of an extensive boom in mineral and oil extraction. Not only were the diamond mines contributing to territorial income, but the region was now the world's leader in money spent and invested in looking for more sources of oil, gas, and minerals. Prospectors, policy makers, and everyday people alike were anxiously anticipating the future benefits of Arctic resources. One national newspaper described the situation this way:

> The 100,000 or so people living in Canada's three northern territories are in the middle of an economic transformation. Emerging economies hungry for raw materials are helping drive growth in the mining

sector. The communications revolution has brought the Arctic closer
to the rest of the world. Native populations are taking advantage of
land-claim settlements to stake their own economic claims. Economi-
cally, the North is heating up. (Ibbitson 2010)

The NWT diamond story is set within this larger narrative of "Arctic
transformation." Intensive state policy realignments, global interest in
Northern resources, climate change debates, questions of Arctic sovereignty, and legacies of colonialism have drawn national and international attention northwards (Byers 2009; Hanrahan 2017; Stuhl 2016;
Todd 2016; Tuck 2014; Wilson and Stammler 2016). While the trope
of a "New North" is not new (Stuhl 2013), journalistic accounts like
the one above paint renewed interest in natural resources as capable
of righting past wrongs and bringing greater equality and inclusion
through increased technological and economic integration. However,
in the NWT, there were competing diamond stories that were far less
optimistic. There were concerns over the social, cultural, and environmental costs of Northern extraction.

Northern Canada is home to a very diverse population of Indigenous peoples (Dene, Inuit, Inuvialuit, Cree, and Métis), non-Indigenous
Canadians (sometimes referred to as Northerners), and a small but
growing number of immigrants from around the world. There are
glaring disparities in health and wealth between Indigenous and
non-Indigenous Northerners. There has been over a hundred years of
mining in the region. This history has involved the (attempted) dispossession of lands from the original inhabitants (Gaudry 2016), the
often-violent transformation of lifeways of Indigenous people, and
severe environmental degradation, with many abandoned projects
leaving behind "toxic legacies" (Sandlos and Keeling 2016). This tu-
multuous past reached a turning point in the 1960s and 1970s, when
Indigenous groups came together to oppose a proposed pipeline
that was to bring natural gas from the Beaufort Sea southwards for
transfer to global markets. Unfettered access to Northern resources
would be no more. Northern Indigenous peoples were part of one
of Canada's largest social movements to date and effectively halted
extraction (Erasmus 1977; D. Smith 1992).

When diamond deposits were discovered in the mid-1990s, the relationship between ethical diamonds and a supposedly ethical nation

was fragile at best. It wasn't immediately clear that these projects would get necessary local approvals. Fast forward to the 2000s, and mining and prospecting were happening at never-before-seen rates. In a relatively short time, Northern natural resources went from being off the table to being eagerly sold on the global market and displayed at national museums.

Under Pressure is an ethnographic and historic account of how northern Canada came to be a global destination for the extractive industry and what this means for the people who live and work in the region. The story I tell is set in Hay River, a multi-ethnic town that serves as a critical transportation node for extractive industries (diamonds are one among many). The story begins with a focus on a single luxury commodity, diamonds, and how ideas about ethical extraction were put into practice largely through Indigenous job training and employment quotas. From there, the book's focus shifts from diamonds as the subject of the research to diamonds as a prism through which we see the bigger picture of Arctic extraction. Diamonds and everyday life are best understood by the pressures that the past and hopes for the future exert on the present for people in this Northern community.

HIGH RISE

Just north of the sixtieth parallel, Hay River and the adjacent K'atl'odeeche First Nation sit along the shores of the Great Slave Lake and along the namesake Hay River. With abundant fish stocks, the area has long been used by Dene (South Slavey) peoples for summer fishing and winter gatherings (K'atl'odeeche First Nation, n.d.). The region saw abrupt change as of the mid-1900s, when the area became a coveted nexus for emerging transportation networks (road/rail/river) created by the Canadian state to help bring Northern resources out.

Hay River's most visible landmark is a seventeen-story high rise residential tower the developer named Mackenzie Place. Locals simply call it "the High Rise." Mackenzie Place looks like many other North American postwar towers built to deal with urbanization: a concrete rectangle with rows of identical windows and balconies and minimal architectural flourishes (see figure 1.1). If it were in a city, it would likely not catch your attention. In the context of Hay River, the

Figure 1.1. Approaching the Mackenzie Place High Rise.
Source: Photo by Jesse Colin Jackson 2013.

High Rise is a visual anomaly. What strikes a first-time visitor as curious is not the building itself, but rather what is not around it. Most
modern residential towers are in clusters and face other towers. This
one sits on the bank of a river in a small Canadian subarctic town. The
landscape is expansive and flat. With everything else around only one
or two stories high, the building looks like it was left here by accident.
When driving north by car, you can begin to spot the High Rise from
seventy-five kilometres away.

Mackenzie Place is home to a diverse set of working-class people
from a variety of backgrounds: Indigenous (Dene, Inuvialuit, Cree,
Métis), settler, and immigrant. Mackenzie Place was built in the 1960s
on the promise of the proposed Mackenzie Valley pipeline that never
came to pass (Dokis 2016; Erasmus 1977; O'Malley 1976). Since then,
it has been repurposed to house those making a living working in the
extractive industry and the corresponding public sectors.

It is wearing out in ways common for towers of its vintage. The
butter yellow exterior paint is peeling. The windows need to be up-
graded. One of the two elevators is often out of service. There is nothing particularly unique about the building's structure. The balconies

are uncluttered. Through the iron railings you might see a single plastic chair. For most of the year it is much too cold to sit outside. Satellite dishes are affixed to the railings along the southwest side: a modern log growing grey plastic mushrooms.

In 2008, I stood in the lobby of the run-down building staring at plastic white letters that listed the names of tenants who were long gone. As I waited to be let in by the building's rental manager, I read and reread the three posted rules:

NO SMOK1NG IN FR0NT.
NO D0GS.
NO H0T3L R00M.

As I waited for the superintendent's wife, I jingled my car keys in my pocket, hopeful that this move would finally set in motion my research on the effects the diamond boom was having on the area. I was in the High Rise that day trying to find a place to live to begin to study this transformation from the perspective of those living through it. The cream-coloured walls, the peeling linoleum tiles, and a buzzer system that did not work were just as I remembered them.

Five years earlier, I was there under very different circumstances. Then, I was a school teacher who had just arrived to take a job teaching fourth grade in a French-language school. I was transferred to this large (by Northern standards) town from a small village in the high Arctic. My partner had been promoted to principal of one of the schools. High salaries and possibilities for early career advancement often drew many "southern" Canadians like us northwards. We were less motivated by money when we initially relocated from Ottawa to the Arctic. We made the 7,000-kilometre move motivated by a sense that we could "do good."

Settler (non-Indigenous) Canadians often see northern Canada in these terms: as a place to start a career, pay off student loans, and/ or do right by Canada's First Peoples by doing care work (teaching, health care) with a social justice orientation. The latter is part of a larger cultural ethos of benevolence that has been widely critiqued as essential to, and not apart from, colonialism (Furniss 2005; Woolford 2015). Well-intentioned settlers (myself among them) are often aware of this contradiction and sit with their complicity while they find ways to serve an Indigenous-directed future. As I transitioned from teacher to researcher, I was aware that the North had again become my "land of opportunity" as the economic and cultural transformations underway ushered in more interest in academic knowledge about the area.

On that first visit in 2003, we waited in between these same two glass doors for the superintendent, who was going to show us a two-bedroom apartment to rent. Trying to imagine a long, cold, dark winter in the decaying building, I became impatient. "Let's just leave," I said. "There is no way that I am going to live here." We left without seeing an apartment, but we were out of rental options. Housing across Canada's North is extremely expensive and usually in short supply. We would have to buy a house. Not exactly a house, we couldn't afford one of those. A trailer. Not the kind on wheels, but the kind made to look like houses by putting fences around them. Everyone in town was saying now was the time to buy. There was a diamond mine that just opened in the region. It was said to be the first of three. "You can't lose" was a common refrain we heard from school parents when debating our real estate options. And we didn't lose. We bought a small trailer, which rose in price substantially in the two years that we owned it before selling.

The day of my arrival as a researcher, Cindy, the building owner's girlfriend and the property manager, saw me and let me in.

"Holy, you got a lot of stuff! Let me get my son Trevor to help you." Cindy put down the mop she was carrying and hurried around the corner shouting, "Trevor! Come help this university woman with her stuff!" I tried to assure her that I could manage, but she insisted, "It's fine, he's not doing nothing anyhow. He is going back to school soon, though. He has a real good opportunity coming up. He is going to be taking an underground mining class at the college here. There's a lot of good jobs up at those diamond mines, you know."

When Cindy told me about her son's upcoming course in underground diamond mining, I was reassured that my move into the High Rise had not been in vain. I was hoping to meet people trying to make a future through resource work and here was my first possible participant. I was familiar with the course Cindy was referring to. It was the most recent iteration of educational opportunities that were supposed to move local people into high-wage work in mining.

When there is a rise in Northern economic activity, many people move to the region from other parts of Canada and increasingly from around the world. This includes Indigenous people like Cindy and Trevor, who are Cree but not locals. In-migrants usually end up in the small number of peri-urban hubs like Hay River as they are accessible by road and have more, even if slim, choices for rental housing. Trevor and his mother's eager anticipation of the course is the direct result of the intersection between ideas about what makes a good life and corporate efforts to mine and market ethical diamonds on politically turbulent territory.

Trevor appeared dragging a large, stubborn-wheeled metal cart to the front door. He had on baggy jeans and a backwards red New York Yankees hat. On the side of his neck was a small tattoo whose green ink had weathered in a way that made the symbol undecipherable. He silently piled my stuff on the wire bed of the cart and asked, "Eighth floor, right?" In the elevator, my questions about his upcoming mining course are met with one-word answers. I asked him if he is from town. "Me? Am I really from this shit hole? No way. I am from La Ronge, Saskatchewan." Laughing, he added, "Some other shit hole!"

Trevor's home community was a former logging town that had seen the end of the industry. His father moved them to Hay River to work in mine construction. After their divorce, Trevor's father moved to another resource boom region, while Cindy elected to stay behind with her two sons to try and make a living here. Hay River is marked by the vestiges of past resources projects and the industrial rubble they left behind. The area is a mash-up of piles of rusting equipment and stunning lakefront and nearby waterfalls. For many people I spoke to, chasing the good life in Hay River and other resource towns often involves imagining leaving them.

The High Rise was a strategic housing choice to get me closer to the people most closely involved in the processes of extraction. Over time, I came to realize that the building did more than merely house the people who could tell the story of the Northern resource economy. Instead, the building itself is a critical storied element of how extraction comes to make sense for many people.

FROM PRISM TO ARCHITECTURES

When light waves pass through a diamond they slow down significantly. This slowing causes light to bend or refract. When light leaves the diamond, it speeds back up causing the refracted wavelengths to appear split into a rainbow of individual colours. This is called dispersion. It is what allows us to see individual colours that are usually entangled as white light. In this book, I shine an anthropological light on diamond mining in Canada to slow down our attention to Arctic extraction and the idea that rapid change is afoot. This ethnographic and historical slowing will reveal the individual, but related, facets of Arctic extraction and everyday life in a Northern peri-urban town. These facets – national ethics, race, infrastructure, mobility, and aspiration – work together to create what I call "architectures of extraction."

Architecture is commonly used to mean both the process and product of planning and building structures like physical buildings, roads, railways, and bridges. The concept of architectures of extraction begins with that definition. However, it goes beyond the commonsensical understanding to include structures in a broader sense, including political-legal structures such as Indigenous land claims, corporate social responsibility agreements, and differentiated citizenships (identity categories coded in law), as well as what we might call aspirational structures – that is, those things that shape people's embodied experiences of their sociocultural worlds and hopes for the future. The physical, political-legal, and aspirational architectures described in the book are what make diamond mining possible. They are structures that preceded diamond development and will outlive it. They exert social, cultural, and economic pressures that shape how people can and do engage with industry. Architectures of extraction are the outcome of planned intervention into Northern lifeworlds by the Canadian state and foreign extraction companies as well as local responses to the pressures these interventions create. Architecture creates possibilities and limits.

The High Rise, its tenants and their stories led me to think less about diamonds and more about the idea of architectures. Architectures of extraction are the structures that create pressures on the present experience of a mining project. They are the different elements that have been put into place that shape how mining is understood and undertaken in a given place at a given time. Some of these elements may have taken shape long ago, while others are more recent. These elements can include tangible things like roads that access the mine or the construction of workers' housing. Architectures of extraction can also be less tangible things like laws and public perceptions or expectations. As a concept, architectures of extraction widen the focus from single mine sites or particular substances (like diamonds) to much longer processes of social and economic transformation.

The concept of architectures of extraction is particularly useful in the case of Northern regions like the NWT where natural resources have been exploited for over a century and the infrastructures supporting them are entangled and overlapping. While much of the media focused on diamonds, I noticed that those involved in their extraction frequently want to talk about other natural resources. The town of Hay River itself could only be explained by considering the ways that mining, fishing (commercial and subsistence), and fur trapping overlapped, sometimes in concert with one another, other times creating serious conflict. Hay River's development is related to the nearby community of Pine Point, which was built around a lead/zinc mine in the 1960s. The mine closed abruptly in the late 1980s when the company realized the best deposits were under the town site. The town, which boasted many new amenities and infrastructure, was partially burned to the ground. Many of Pine Point's homes were relocated to Hay River. Yet, even with the startling end of Pine Point as a community, the railroad built for that mine which ends in Hay River is indispensable for bringing in the diesel that fuels diamond mining and other ventures. Much in the same way, the High Rise was built for a pipeline that never came. Nevertheless, it is indispensable for the projects that came later (diamonds, among others) and to house people like Cindy, Trevor, and even me.

Since the turn of the twenty-first century, anthropologists have started to investigate the role of infrastructures – both technological and social – in cultural life (Anand 2011; Dourish and Bell 2007; Mains 2012; Star 1999). This begins from the premise that possibilities for the human experience are afforded by infrastructures of all kinds (water pipes, telephone towers, roads). As AbdouMaliq Simone (2012) writes, "Infrastructure exerts a force – not simply in the materials and energies it avails, but also the way it attracts people, draws them in, coalesces and expends their capacities." Part of a broader "material turn" in the humanities, the anthropology of infrastructure displaced some of the human-centric work of traditional anthropology and opened up space to see the intricate connections between human and non-human. The term "infrastructure" generally includes things such as bridges, roads, electric grids, water systems, and networks. In short, infrastructure is basic physical systems and foundational services for cities, neighbourhoods, buildings, and facilities.

I am building on the anthropology of infrastructure but elect to use the term "architecture" as it is more expansive and brings together the art and science of design. What matters with infrastructure is largely that it works. Think about water pipes. It matters that they bring water and not so much what they look like. With architecture, our judgments are about function but often rely on much more. Does the style reflect personal and societal values, aspirations, and sense of self or place? While infrastructure is also necessarily aesthetic (Larkin 2018), architecture does a better job of keeping an eye on both structure as well as design and artifice, elements that are essential to understanding the Arctic's transformation. In chapter 4, you will see how the High Rise was an emblem of imposed modernization and all that is wrong with expedited development. These past feelings of dissatisfaction animate the way people debate the future of not only the High Rise but the community more broadly.

The attention I paid to the town of Hay River, the town's sole High Rise building, its history, and the tenants who came and went over the decade of writing this book are what led me to see and understand diamonds through their necessary architectures. Architecture, like infrastructure, creates possibilities and pressures at the same time. Instead of passing judgment on mining as either good for economic development or a disastrous "slow industrial genocide" (Huseman and Short 2012), I outline how diamond mining is woven into the everyday lives of some of the people living in the region. I ask: how does mining, for many people, make sense? How did Arctic extraction become enmeshed with people's views of their futures?

THINKING ABOUT EXTRACTION ANTHROPOLOGICALLY

Coming up with ways to understand the complexity of mining's impacts on society is critical, as the contemporary production and consumption of mineral resources has now outpaced anything we have ever witnessed historically (Arsel, Hogenboom, and Pellegrini 2016;

Jacka 2018, 62). My interest in mining and resource development builds on a long history of anthropological interest in extraction (Nash 1979). Founding work in the area focused on the economics of large-scale mines, as well as the social organization and ritual and ideology of mining communities (Godoy 1985; Jorgensen 1997; Taussig 1980).

One way that anthropological approaches differ from other approaches is that we believe "natural" resources are in fact deeply cultural (Ferry and Limbert 2008; Haraway 1997; Latour 1993). They don't merely exist in the world; rather, it is human desires and use that bring them into being as valuable objects (Ferry 2013; Walsh 2010). As anthropologists Tanya Richardson and Gisa Weszkalnys put it, "natural resources are inherently *distributed things* whose essence or character is to be located neither exclusively in their biophysical properties nor in webs of socio-cultural meanings" (Richardson and Weszkalnys 2014, 8). This approach forces us to keep an eye on both the social and material qualities of natural resources. To understand diamonds is to consider how their specific physical characteristics are interwoven with Western cultural understandings of them as rare and precious objects.

When Northern diamonds were discovered in the 1990s, mining in general had a poor public image and stock prices were sinking.[1] Diamonds, as you will see in chapter 2, had a particularly tarnished imaged due to their connection to armed conflicts in Sierra Leone and the Democratic Republic of Congo. As a result, new forms of corporate social responsibility (CSR) were put in place to attempt to redeem the industry's image. CSR is a broad term for policies that guide a

---

1 The turn to the twenty-first century saw many countries in the Global South pressured by international agencies like the World Bank and the International Monetary Fund to liberalize their mining sectors through privatization and deregulation (Jacka 2018). Extractive projects began to disproportionately take shape on Indigenous land. At the same time, countries like Canada and Australia de-nationalized their local mining efforts and became more attractive sites for investors. Since its inception as a colonial country, Canada has had mining-friendly policies through what is called the free-entry system (Hoogeveen 2014). "The free entry gives mining companies the exclusive right to Crown-owned mineral substances from the surface of their claim to an unlimited extension downwards" (Campbell 2004). This system, and the settler colonial ethos that underpins it, has been heavily criticized in Canada and Australia (Hoogeveen 2014; Howlett and Lawrence 2019; Moreton-Robinson 2015). Most notably, "free entry" denies Indigenous land tenure. Between Indigenous rights violations and environmental concerns, global criticisms of the mining industry were mounting.

corporation's relationship to the places and people it relies on for its products. In step with industry changes, the anthropology of mining has moved its ethnographic focus to CSR and the growing number of mediating institutions (NGOs, consultancies) and legal apparatuses (environmental and social assessments, impact-benefit agreements) that govern community-corporate relationships.

Much of the research in social science has been critical of CSR as a kind of greenwashing or smoke screen to allow for rapid, unsustainable development (Gilberthorpe and Banks 2012; Hilson 2006; Jacka 2015; Sharp 2006). Anthropologists have added to these conversations by first showing that even if CSR is a global phenomenon, it takes shape in local communities in drastically different ways (Coumans 2011; Rajak 2009; Sawyer 2004; Welker 2009, 2012). Local people can and do shape the ways in which mining projects come to pass, or not (F. Li 2009). Perhaps more importantly, anthropological approaches show that notions of "community" and "corporation" are not so straightforward (Welker 2014). In his book on gold mining in Papua New Guinea, Alex Golub (2014) illustrates how "the mine" and "the Ipili" (a local Indigenous group) were brought into being in relation to one another and how certain individuals were authorized to speak for the mine and others to speak for the Ipili. This kind of nuance is often overlooked in popular, critical, or activist accounts. This makes it essential to study the relationship between a global industry and local people in a way that encompasses the complexity of the situation.

INDIGENEITY, ANTHROPOLOGY, AND THE ARCTIC

For clarity, I want to explain my choice of words like Aboriginal, Indigenous, and related terms. Wherever I can, I use the term the specific people I am talking about would use to describe themselves. Sometimes that word is a broad ethnic category like Dene, Inuvialuit, or Métis. They may use "Native," "Aboriginal," or "Indian," but unless it is a direct quote, I don't use these terms as they have derogatory connotations when used by non-Indigenous people. The term "First Nations," which is used widely in other parts of Canada, is not used here, except in reference to the physical location of the community adjacent to Hay River (and less so the group of people). Rarely do people in the NWT use "Indigenous" to talk about themselves; however, this is starting to shift. There is still a strong preference for "Aboriginal" in the region. Nevertheless, when talking more generally about issues having to do with Indigeneity, I use "Indigenous" to gesture to the largest, most inclusive set of people in the area rather than to any one specific group or region.

Anthropology in North America was historically the science of Indigenous "Others" (Deloria Jr. 1969; A. Simpson 2014). The Arctic was of particular interest to key figures like Franz Boas as there was a belief that the most isolated groups held more "pure" or distinct culture. The part of the world that I explore in this book was often dismissed by anthropologists in the early 1900s as having "no good culture left" (Mason 1946). Multi-ethnic Arctic communities like Hay River are critical nodes in global extractive networks; however, the anthropology of Arctic extraction has typically focused on small Indigenous villages and has been interested in questions about the past or about relationships to place. When questions about the nature of community-corporate relationships are taken up, there is a tendency to create caricatures of each side, often erasing the nuance and complexity of the situation (Bielawski 2004; Dokis 2016; Hall 2022). This can be politically useful, even necessary. Without a doubt, what underwrites Arctic mining is the history and present of colonial policies and logics set forth by the British Empire and now the Canadian state (Mackey 2016; Todd 2020).

Indigenous legal scholars Glen Coulthard and Leanne Betasamosake Simpson (2016) define settler colonialism as "a structure of domination that is partly predicated on the ongoing dispossession of Indigenous peoples' lands and the forms of political authority and jurisdiction that govern our relationship to these lands" (251; see also Coulthard 2014). Settler colonialism is a structure, not an event (Wolfe 1999; Todd 2017), meaning it is an ongoing practice and not a fixed historical moment in the past. As such, Indigenous scholars are making it clear that Northern research should be in Northern hands (Moffitt, Chetwynd, and Todd 2015). With good reason, Indigenous scholars globally continue to be wary of non-Indigenous researchers and of anthropology. Mohawk scholar Audra Simpson writes,

> In different moments, anthropology has imagined itself to be a voice,
> and in some disciplinary iterations, the voice of the colonized (Said

1989; Paine 1990). This modern interlocutionary role had a serious material and ideational context; it accorded the imperatives of Empire and in this, specific technologies of rule that sought to obtain space and resources, to define and know the difference that it constructed in those spaces, and to then govern those within (Asad 1979; Said [1978] 1994, 1989). Knowing and representing people within those places required more than military might; it required the methods and modalities of knowing – in particular, categorization, ethnological comparison, linguistic translation, and ethnography. (A. Simpson 2014, 95)

By anchoring the reader's attention to the architectures of Northern "development" and how people live within them, I keep the focus on the processes that affect ordinary Northern people's lives in often mundane but important ways (a broken elevator when you are late for work). I concur with Indigenous scholars that knowledge production "about" Indigenous people and their beliefs and legal orders is best done by and for themselves (Gaudry 2011; First Nations Information Governance Centre 2014). My intention in this book is to shift the focus of the gaze such that Indigenous people are not the object of analysis; rather, the research problem is global extraction and colonialism. These are two entangled forces that depend on Indigenous people in multiple, complex ways.

It is important to be clear here that this is not an anthropology of an Indigenous group or groups, and the people with whom I engage in the coming pages are not meant as representations of some larger homogeneous ethnic whole. Quite the contrary. People like Trevor and Cindy are both migrant and Indigenous and therefore not the kind of people who would not be consulted about a mine's effects or interviewed for their local knowledge. While I spoke with many people, whose identities are multiple and sometimes include Indigeneity, I make no claim that I "speak for" them. Rather, I hope their experiences "speak to" how settler colonialism is experienced on the ground.

There are many difficult, and likely imperfect, choices I made to try and write ethnographically in the context of settler colonialism. The approach I take here follows on the heels of work done by Australian/settler anthropologists who target their attention to settler policies and practices that constitute Indigenous Australians as a problem to be solved (Lea 2020; Lea and Pholeros 2010; Wolfe 1999). This work unpacks the logics and workings of settler colonialism as a paradigm that serves itself even as it claims to serve others (Lea 2008). While perhaps the work could be thought of as fitting within the frame of Settler Colonial Studies (Veracini 2011), my approach does not satisfy calls to "decolonize anthropology" (Harrison 1991, 1997; Mogstad and Tse 2018). There are Indigenous scholars who outline concrete ways to begin such an exercise (Todd 2018; Tuck and Yang 2012), including leaving/abolishing anthropology altogether (Todd 2020) and developing anticolonial scientific practice more broadly (Liboiron 2021).

To date, there is exceptional research on remote Northern Indigenous communities confronting extractive mega-projects (Bielawski 2004; Cater 2017; Dokis 2016; Hall 2022) as well as important Indigenous theoretical critiques of the forms of Indigenous recognition that accompany these economic interests (Coulthard 2014; Tuck 2014). *Under Pressure* aims to add another facet to these discussions by holding Indigenous rights and migrant and immigrant experiences in the same analytical frame. Living in the High Rise allowed me to explore the legacies of colonialism through the unlikely lens of a settler structure. In line with many Indigenous recommendations for research methods (Gaudry 2011; Jimmy, Andreotti, and Stein 2019; Tuck and Yang 2012), this book focuses neither on sacred Indigenous knowledge (which isn't mine to collect or circulate) and cultural difference (Moreton-Robinson 2015), nor on the difficulties of endurance (Povinelli 2008) that mark many, but not all, Indigenous lives. My focus instead is on a global process and not "a people." *Under Pressure* is my attempt to grapple ethnographically and analytically with resource extraction in ways that enrich, rather than flatten, how settler Canadians and other non-Northerners understand Northern lifeworlds.

METHODS AND OTHER NOTES

I came to the term "architecture of extraction" in the way that most anthropologists build theory and concepts – that is, through long-term fieldwork in a place that exemplifies the process in which I was interested. The research for this book was intentionally multi-sited. It includes interviews and observations at mining industry events in major Canadian cities like Toronto, Vancouver, and the NWT capital of Yellowknife. However, the bulk of the account I offer here is based on extended work in the multi-ethnic (Indigenous, settler, immigrant) community of Hay River (population 4,000). The historical and geographical context of this community matters to the story I offer here.

Data for this book come from twenty months of fieldwork conducted over a four-year period. I began the work by understanding and unpacking discourses that promoted mine development. I collected relevant policy documents and spoke to people in the industry (usually off the record, at their insistence) and listened to panels on anything related to human resources and/or Indigenous/community relationships. I developed a research proposal that I sent to local Indigenous groups for review as part of the research licensing process. From there, I began surveying the educational terrain by taking stock of the opportunities for training and interviewing those responsible for delivering and designing these programs. I toured training facilities in the capital and then relocated to Hay River, where I had the strongest relationships. I spent time in educational settings, getting to know program participants and interviewing them once their courses ended. Once I moved into the High Rise, I got to know residents and engaged many in formal interviews. In the lobby, I posted signs to explain who I was and why I was there. However, it was my dog, a droopy but energetic basset hound, who got most conversations started.

There were other means of knowing that are more difficult to articulate. This stems from my relationship to the community of Hay River, which is layered and not easy to describe succinctly. Often researchers from outside a community have trouble shedding their identity as researchers. For those who are members of the community, holding multiple roles and responsibilities can be a challenge. My position was perhaps unique in that I had lived in the community as a teacher; I then left to pursue graduate degrees in Northern and Indigenous education and then returned as an ethnographer. As costs of living are high, I took a contract teaching half days at the French school and began leading popular evening aerobics classes. These activities subsidized fieldwork that would have otherwise not been possible on a graduate student stipend. In the interim between leaving and my return, I lost a lot of weight. Between my different body size and the aerobics classes, most people in town thought of me as "the Jazzercise lady." Women in town wanted primarily to talk to me about diet and exercise. I had a difficult time steering conversations in other directions, especially with middle-class people. The other change that didn't go unnoticed was the end of my long-term relationship with the school principal. She and I were still amicable and there was a lot of curiosity about whether we would reunite (no) and whether or not I was "still gay" (it's complicated). For years, these facets of my personal history felt like an obstacle to my success as a researcher. I would learn things relevant to my project at social events and then had to consider how to ethically document the details or, more often, decide to exclude them. Even when conversations were explicitly begun as "interviews" the shift to more personal modes of relating left me feeling like what I was learning was not to be shared. These tense internal debates are familiar territory to anthropologists, but at the time I experienced them as very isolating. My field site was neither at "home" nor was it totally "away" (even if on unceded Indigenous land). This messy middle was both an asset and a partial obstacle to my role as a researcher and is worth being explicit about.

Hay River is a very small town by most standards. As such, I have done what many ethnographers do to help conceal the identities of their participants. I use pseudonyms for everyone I write about. In some rare cases, I have created composites of multiple people whose accounts speak to the same points I am making. At other junctures I have changed any detail that would be too immediately recognizable to local readers. That said, some readers will be able to identify the people in these pages. This is something people knew in speaking to me. I could never guarantee anonymity in such a tightly knit place.

ARCHITECTURE OF A DIAMOND STORY

No one person or company can fully control the stories that shape diamonds' meanings. In chapter 2, "Nation," you will learn how and why the story of diamonds as an emblem of love and romance was in jeopardy in the late 1990s. The expansion of large-scale mining globally was matched by new kinds of globalized activism (Kirsch 2007; Rajak 2011). Sensing the rise in opposition, mining mega-corporation

Rio Tinto gathered industry leaders to improve public opinion and put forth the notion of "sustainable mining" (Kirsch 2010, 2014). This turn of events ushered in new corporate social responsibility (CSR) practices and policies that shaped the future of mining in northern Canada. The chapter will illustrate how competing meanings of Canada shaped CSR and the new Northern diamond story. It explains how Indigenous employment came to take up so much discursive space in the public diamond story and created the mining course that Cindy was so optimistic about for her son Trevor. However, Northern CSR measures tend to oversimplify the Northern diamond story, reinforcing a very truncated view of time, space, and race as they relate to the consequences of resource extraction. The remainder of the book moves beyond the narrow terms of debate set out by industry and government through CSR measures by focusing on everyday life in Hay River.

The High Rise will become the narrative anchor to illustrate a bigger picture. It was there that I met Destiny, a young Dene woman also enrolled in the course Trevor was looking forward to. In chapter 3, "Race," I weave her experiences of resource-related activity with those of an Indigenous man living in the area in the 1870s. I encountered his name, John Hope, through archival research done locally and at the archives of the Hudson's Bay Company in Winnipeg. This chapter establishes race and space as the foundation of the architecture of extraction in the North by showing how ideas of race/Indigeneity changed over time in relationship to different extractive ambitions on the part of the Canadian state. Once specific architectures of race, place, and property were set in motion, the necessary infrastructure for resource development could take shape.

Chapter 4, "Infrastructure," uses the history of the High Rise itself to discuss state-led Northern "modernization" efforts that ramped up in the 1960s in the interest of increasing access to oil, uranium, and other minerals. I describe how the town of Hay River was designed as a "gateway to the North" on the heels of a pipeline that never came to pass. I show how infrastructure from past projects (even failed ones) comes to animate contemporary concerns over mining futures.

Mappings of race and space described in chapter 2 and infrastructure described in chapter 3 not only worked to link people to place but also served, somewhat counterintuitively, to enable substantial in-migration. Mobilities of different scales are essential components in the architecture of extraction. While there is a concerted effort to understand mining's impacts on Indigenous people (Gilberthorpe and Hilson 2016; Hall 2022), the same level of attention has not been paid to in/out-migration of people from across Canada and around the world. These issues are inseparable. The High Rise is home to a diverse set of people from a variety of ethnic and class backgrounds. Some, like Destiny, are from nearby, while others arrive from distant parts of the globe or the other side of Canada. Chapter 5, "Mobility," shares stories of several tenants and what brought them to the building, as well as their hopes to leave it. It describes national, international, and local forms of migration that are central to, but never fully managed by, the extractive industry. The tenant trajectories show how labour mobility in and out of the region is an essential element in the architecture of extraction.

In-migration over the latter half of the twentieth century increased competition for resources of various kinds (fish, caribou, wage work). These shifts made it increasingly difficult for Indigenous people to live in the ways they had for the better part of a century. Broken promises over guaranteed hunting and fishing rights alongside the rise in a parallel cash economy meant that Indigenous access to wage work became necessary for survival. Although Indigenous people had always been central to extractive industries (guiding, procuring foodstuffs, providing local knowledge, labour), their exclusion from higher-wage stable employment became an increasing point of contention. When the diamond mines were proposed, local people wanted guarantees that advertised work would go to them.

Chapter 6, "Morality," follows Trevor and Destiny from the High Rise to the state-industry training program they eagerly awaited. Delivered at the local community college, the first course in the sequence was in "soft skills" training. Through participant-observation in the course and interviews with ten students, I describe how the course aimed to teach habits and aspirations that aligned with corporate values against the backdrop of corporate social responsibility campaigns that placed a high premium on Indigenous participation in the industry. When the global financial crisis reached north of sixty degrees midway through my extended fieldwork, much of the advertised work disappeared. Course values such as "responsibility" and "having a good attitude" became paramount in managing local disappointment and possible opposition.

Aspiration is not unique to the underemployed. In chapter 7, "Aspiration," I show how the emergence and maintenance of a Northern middle class is essential to the architecture of extraction and yet has not been discussed in academic settings. While extractive industry created an expanded middle class and peri-urbanization, you will see how and why being middle class isn't so straightforward for everyone. At the centre of this chapter are Métis middle-class women who moved up and out of the High Rise and have since developed intricate structures for creating arm's-length ways of making resource futures for themselves and their families.

Nation, race, infrastructure, mobility, morality, and aspiration are the architectural facets that enabled diamond mining to take shape in the way that it did in the Northwest Territories in the 2000s. Without any of one of these elements, the structure may have collapsed. That is not to say they are all stable, as you will see over the course of the book. If you were to see Foxfire, or any Northern diamond, for yourself all of these architectural elements would be invisible. We often take for granted the wide range of social, political, economic, and historical forces that bring commodities into being. We have a sense that things are made or mined, but the wide-reaching conditions that make the things we love and cherish possible are hard to see in a quick glance. By taking diamonds as an anthropological prism, the pressures, paths, and possibilities for Trevor, Cindy, Destiny, and others in this book are dispersed and the individual architectures that sustain them revealed.

DISCUSSION QUESTIONS

1 Before you begin the chapter, brainstorm in writing or by drawing what comes to mind when you think of northern Canada
   or the Arctic. After reading the chapter, consider how the book
   reinforces your expectations or complicates them.

2 The High Rise is described as a visual anomaly. In his book, *Indians in Unexpected Places* (2004), Sioux historian Philip Deloria
   writes that anomalies are windows into our broad cultural expectations. We name an anomaly in relation to accepted norms
   and categories. Anomalies and expectations are therefore mutu-
   ally constitutive. By naming something an anomaly, we reinforce
   the very expectations and categories the anomaly is said to be
   breaking. Consider something you have seen that you would
   describe as anomalous. What makes it so? What are the expectations that underpin the idea of the anomaly? What categories
   does the anomaly depend on to work?

3 Think of a memorable example of architecture that you have
   seen. What are the qualities that draw you to it? Does it reflect
   your values in some way? Does it reflect the surrounding community's values or interrupt them in any way?

4 According to the author, what is the difference between architecture and infrastructure? How do you understand these two
   terms?

5 Find the closest active resource extraction site to your community. Find media coverage related to the site and describe the recurring themes presented in the media. What, if anything, would
   an anthropological perspective add to public discourse?

CHAPTER TWO

Nation

NOTHING BUT PROBLEMS

When I began the research for this book in 2007, Canada was the third-largest producer of diamonds by value in the world (Statistics Canada 2007). The designation "by value" means that Canada did not produce the third-largest volume of stones; rather, it signals that stones from Canada were sold at higher market prices than their competitors. This increased value was created by their marketing as ethical alternatives to "blood diamonds." Blood diamonds are gemstones from countries like Sierra Leone, Angola, and the Democratic Republic of Congo. These particular diamonds became icons of unethical consumption in the early 2000s when global activist campaigns drew oversimplified attention to connections between armed conflict and the diamond trade. Although mined by transnational extraction companies like Rio Tinto, De Beers, and BHP Billiton, diamonds from the Northwest Territories are branded as "Canadian" to offer consumers a purchase that is purportedly free of conflict. Diamonds from the Canadian Arctic are promoted as empowering local (Indigenous) peoples through business partnerships, job training, and employment. Trevor's upcoming course was part of corporate efforts to share the benefits of extraction with Indigenous people.

Once I began this research, the issue of ethical diamonds seemed to follow me wherever I went. Over the winter holidays of 2008, I was home in Toronto on a break from the "field" (meaning the NWT). I was hurriedly holiday shopping at a local mall when I realized respite from my research could not be counted on. I was in a retail chain jewellery store looking for a gift for a confirmation I was attending when I went back north. As the salesman tried to help me choose from a rotating Plexiglas cabinet of gold crosses, I mentioned I was buying the gift to take back to the Northwest Territories. His eyes grew wide with excitement. "We have your diamonds!" he said, shuttling me away from the case of golden crosses to the middle of the store. In a frameless glass box, loose piles of sparkling stones slept on black velvet. In the background, the iconic red maple leaf knit together two words printed in bold white letters: CANADIAN DIAMONDS.

"Hmm. Yes. The diamonds…," I hesitated.

Sensing my skepticism, he interjected, "Are you an environmentalist or something?"

As a woman social scientist interested in mining, I was used to people's suspicion of me being an environmentalist or a "greenie." "No, it's just that I write about the social impacts of the resource development in the north, and, well…."

"Yeah, well and what?" Now his tone was hurried and abrupt. He continued, "I hear there's nothing but problems up there. The diamond industry makes a lot of jobs for the Native people. What's wrong with that?"

The phrase "nothing but problems" is a casual, albeit powerful, quality of life assessment. Such assessments evoke ideas about human suffering that equate ethnicity (in this case, Indigeneity) with a host of ambiguous social problems. It then makes sense of these problems by bracketing them off and understanding them as in the process of resolution. The resolution in progress, or said differently, the future which we are to orient Others to, is wage work in the primary sector. The notion that Indigenous people are either suffering from extraction or can be saved by it are commonsensical positions for many settler Canadians. In many ways, these oversimplified visions of the Arctic are what motivated me to do this work.

The inaccuracy and inappropriateness of the salesperson's comments aside, I want to draw attention to the assumed relationship between ethical consumption, Canada, and Indigenous quality of life.

This chapter outlines the ethical pressures on the diamond industry and the Canadian nation-state that give shape to the architecture of extraction. The chapter begins by outlining international and national industry criticisms and then describing the corporate social responsibility (CSR) practices that were put into place as a result. I show how Canadian nationalism is both an asset and a threat to Northern diamonds' value as ethical objects. More importantly, I argue that CSR and related discourses promote a chronotopically constrained view of extraction that makes Arctic issues such as resource wealth and Indigenous poverty harder rather than easier to understand. Said differently, CSR tends to picture extraction in very narrow terms with respect to physical space and time. These industry-driven methods of shoring up local support for mining are what make the jewellery salesperson's comments possible.

MAKING DIAMONDS CANADIAN

Diamonds from Canada are part of a rapidly growing commodity class: ethical commodities. James Carrier (2010) defines "ethical commodities" as material objects infused with value-producing moral attributes that can be assessed by the purchaser. Said more plainly, they are things that we attach moral ideas to that in turn raise the price of the object. For commodities to be understood as "ethical," they must be rendered legible. That is, there must be a means by which a consumer can distinguish between two objects with identical physical properties. Designations like "fair trade" or "conflict-free" are meant to create this distinction by making it legible to consumers. Making ethics legible isn't as straightforward as applying a label. Canadian diamonds gained their ethical status in part through their contrast to African-mined stones and artisanal mining methods. By focusing on their national point of origin (Canada), marketing materials could semiotically hitchhike on notions of Canada as fair and democratic. This set of meanings is contested, however, as Indigenous-state relations in Canada are vexed and ongoing legacies of colonialism are a topic of national and local political concern.

The ethical framing of diamonds from Canada depended in part on how other sources of diamonds became "unethical" on the international stage. In 2001, global NGO World Vision launched a human rights campaign to "bring clarity to the diamond sector." The campaign drew global attention to a relationship between African diamonds and armed conflicts in countries like Sierra Leone, Angola, and the Democratic Republic of Congo. The campaigns asked consumers to help put an end to the circulation of what became shorthanded as "blood diamonds." Campaigns and exposés on issues associated with "blood diamonds" took many forms: consumer-targeted ads, documentary films, non-fiction accounts, and a Hollywood blockbuster. In the television documentary *Diamond Road* (Pahuja and Becker 2007), shoeless diamond diggers in Sierra Leone wade through murky waters in the small hopes that they might find a valuable stone. The documentary goes on to show that even if a diamond is found, the chain of exploitation is such that the digger receives little reward. Images of artisanal alluvial diggers gained prominence in the global diamond imaginary through visuals like these (Falls 2011).[1]

As the counterimage to African "darkness" (Ferguson 2006), Canadian diamonds were marketed as "white stones" and "pure ice." These terms are loaded with symbolic value: whereas blood runs hot, ice runs cold. Ice occurs naturally, whereas blood is drawn in the realms of the sociopolitical. Most advertisements emphasized notions of whiteness and purity by drawing on images of untouched snowy northern landscapes and using slogans like "as pure and beautiful as the Arctic itself" (Canada Diamonds, n.d.). Many print advertisements use Arctic icons such as glaciers and polar bears to evoke imaginaries of the far North, even if the mines are landlocked (meaning not near glaciers) and only 150–400 kilometres outside of the capital city of Yellowknife in a bio-zone better described as taiga than tundra (meaning no polar bears).

Through "blood diamonds" campaigns, "African" stones were infused with qualities of immorality. The presence of these qualities, then, could be either confirmed or negated by a responsible consumer. When diamond mogul De Beers became the target of many campaigns to raise awareness against conflict stones, their well-known

---

1 In her essay "Picturing Blood Diamonds," Falls (2011) examines these campaigns. The major NGOs involved in picturing blood diamonds include Global Witness, Partnership Africa Canada, and Amnesty International.

advertising slogans proved particularly vulnerable to the critical adaptations that rendered certain stones "unethical." Ad spoofs like "diamonds are a guerrilla's best friend" or "amputation is forever" (Falls 2011) were accompanied by gruesome images that evoked a "grammar of responsibility" (Barnett et al. 2011) that held the consumer in the particularly powerful subject position of disciplining the diamond industry generally or the individual corporations specifically (but never the wider process of exploitation). As it would turn out, diamonds' emergent grammar of responsibility coincided with, and was amplified by, a new site for procuring the precious stone: the Canadian Arctic. One prominent campaign suggested that the four Cs of diamond selection criteria (cut, colour, clarity, and carat) should be joined by a fifth.

> Think of how much you pay for a diamond. One diamond alone can purchase many weapons. If you're buying a diamond, don't forget to ask about the fifth "C" – Does this diamond come from a conflict zone? And tell your friends to do likewise. Concerned consumers will help keep the industry honest. (Hart 2002, 187; quoted in Grant and Taylor 2004)

Diamond development supporters in Canada felt the emerging industry was best placed to "secure a premium from the 'peacefulness and integrity' of its mining context" (McCarthy 2003; quoted in Le Billon 2006). Some of the most enthusiastic supporters went as far as to suggest that the fifth "C" of diamond selection criteria should be "Canadian." Consumer-directed advertisements oriented ethical concerns towards the diamonds' country of origin and thus nationalized the diamonds from the Northwest Territories. In the process, the NWT was conflated with Canada, thus collapsing some of the key historical, political, and cultural particularities of the region. Diamonds from Canada also faced the challenge of becoming legible as distinctly different from their "conflict" counterparts. By highlighting the country of origin (Canada) in promotional materials and sales interactions, diamonds' ethical value is inflated (at least in Canadian markets).

According to the Canadian Diamond Code of Conduct (2002), stones are said to be "Canadian" if they are mined in Canada. Cutting and polishing can, and does, happen abroad. In large part, stones are cut and polished in India or China, then taken to Belgium to be resold. While there was a heavily state-subsidized attempt to set up a cutting and polishing industry in the NWT, almost all facilities were closed during the financial crisis. The majority of producers of finished so-called Canadian diamond jewellery keep their production process outside of Canada. I interviewed one of the leading producers of Canadian diamond jewellery who explained that the bulk of their pieces are made in Merida, Mexico. Only the occasional commissioned piece is manufactured in Toronto. In *Capital Volume I*, Marx (1992) is concerned with how commodities tend to be presented or perceived in a peculiar way under capitalism. This method of representation ignores or denies the labour time entailed in the commodities' production and (re)presentation to the would-be purchaser. He calls this "the fetishism of commodities and the secret thereof." Although "Canadian" signals some attention to the labour power required to mine stones (it indicates that the diamonds are not the result of poor working conditions such as those endured by alluvial miners in Africa), it also obscures forms of labour involved in the process, such as cutting, polishing, and setting. Even in the case of ethical commodities that make production (partially) transparent through certification processes, "fetishism," broadly conceived, helps to maintain a focus on the general tendency to obscure the wide range of relations that bring objects to market (Carrier 2010).[2]

The production of Canadian diamonds largely happens beyond the country's borders. More to the point, none of the companies in operation during my core fieldwork were Canadian owned, although many are traded on the Toronto Stock Exchange. Many Canadian-owned mining extraction firms operate abroad. While many North American exploration capital firms invest at home, seldom do extraction firms pursue local projects. North America is unfavourable when compared

---

2 Carrier (2010), using basic principles of semiotics, adds that eventually the instance can come to replace the category itself. For instance, if packages of "ethical" coffee have photographs of smiling small-scale farmers, then eventually "ethical" coffee *must* be produced by small-scale farmers. This is problematic, as it obscures matters like small-scale farmers' inability to meet production demand and relying on iterant/migrant labour (West 2012). This holds true in the Canadian case. National "ethical consumers" often say "it's Canadian" to index a morally superior, even if highly ambiguous, choice.

to the "less developed" world (Tsing 2005). Often complaining that Canadian regulatory regimes are too cumbersome or inhospitable to free-market logic, transnational mining corporations (TMCs) prefer those states that expedite time between discovery and production. As Anna Tsing (2000, 2005) explains, "By the 1980s, the locus [of Canadian mining] had shifted from mining *in* Canada to mining *for* Canada" or, perhaps more precisely, for Canadian capital markets (Tsing 2000, 139, my emphasis). Nationalizing diamonds as Canadian products erases large parts of the investment, production, and circulation processes.

Canadian diamonds are global products. Yet their nationality matters a great deal to consumers interested in making ethical purchases. The issue of "origin" is not itself sufficient in making ethical claims legible. There is always the possibility that local people could make counterclaims to corporate ethics. In the case of the NWT, outstanding Indigenous land claims issues jeopardize the idea that these diamonds are not harmful to human beings.

In the 1990s, at the time of diamond discovery, the proposed mines were located on land that was under dispute between the government and various Indigenous groups. The region, known to onlookers as the "barren lands,' is northeast of Great Slave Lake. Building the first mine required draining Lac De Gras (fat lake) as the mineral deposits were thought to be richest at the bottom. The closest communities to the mines are Łutselk'e, a village of 300, and Yellowknife, the capital city that is traditionally Dene but now has an ethnically mixed population of almost 20,000. As a result, the focus of the mine's potential impacts focused on these two locales at the early stages of development. At that time, previous legal rulings held that all extractive activity was supposed to be suspended until land negotiations between the federal government and Indigenous groups were complete. Nevertheless, the government approved the first mine on the condition that the corporation make "significant progress in sixty days" in its relationships with the nearest Indigenous communities (Bielawski 2004).

Anthropologist Ellen Bielawski worked in the community of Łutselk'e during what is best described as the sixty-day scramble. She documents the endless bureaucratic meetings and how the local leadership tried to come to grips with the ramifications of the mega-project. She describes the community members as having a range of reactions, from hopeful for employment prospects to decidedly against the project. She asserts that the sentiment was that the mine was a foregone conclusion and so the next best thing was to ensure that the community benefited. Speaking to then-chief of the Yellowknives Dene First Nation, Darrell Beaulieu, about previous encounters with extractive industry, she quotes him as saying, "[T]he government got royalties, the shareholders got their cash, and the First Nations got the shaft" (Bielawski 2004, 158). New kinds of corporate-Indigenous agreements were intended by Canada's settler state to change this pattern and ensure that the mine's reputations could reflect the Canadian ethos of non-harm. The need to ensure community support alongside the imperative to stand apart from "blood diamonds" amplified initiatives that were already underway in the extractive industries: corporate social responsibility.

MAKING CANADIAN DIAMONDS

To fully explain how the national and international ethics campaigns took the shape that they did, I need to share some basic facts about diamonds and how they are mined. Diamonds are a carbon allotrope whose natural formation requires rather specific conditions, chiefly high pressure and low temperature. They form far below Earth's surface and are carried upwards by deep-originating volcanic eruptions. The magma travelling up the volcanic pipe cools into igneous rock known as kimberlite or lamproite (Erlich and Hausel 2002). Not all kimberlite pipes are necessarily diamondiferous. Prospectors rely on easier-to-spot indicator minerals such as (red) garnet, (black) ilmenite, and (green) olivine, which tend to co-occur with diamonds. Primary source diamonds are those that are still embedded in kimberlite. Secondary source diamonds, often called alluvial diamonds, are those that have eroded out of their kimberlite or lamproite matrix and accumulated because of water or wind action. These different sources dictate different harvesting methods.

Alluvial diamond mining is the term used to describe the process through which diamonds are recovered from secondary sources such as deposits of sand, gravel, or clay in riverbeds or shorelines. Alluvial diamond deposits are not usually mined industrially as they are spread across huge geographic areas that cannot be easily isolated.

These diamond deposits are usually exploited through artisanal or small-scale alluvial diamond digging. So-called conflict stones are generally mined in this way.[3]

Primary source diamonds, on the other hand, must be mined industrially. They are significantly more capital intensive, but arguably less labour intensive. Diamonds mined in Canada fall into this category. They are mined primarily using open-pit or open-cast methods. This process involves creating a large hole in the ground with explosives. Heavy equipment digs out and collects ore, which is then taken to an on-site processing and recovery plant. This ore then passes through several machines that separate diamonds from other matter using a variety of chemical and technical methods. Once the ore is in the processing stage, it is tracked by a handful of workers who observe the process via computer screens in an office. The division of labour, combined with the intense security measures and procedures, means that very few employees come into physical contact with Arctic diamonds.

The value of diamonds mined using open-pit methods is measured in carats per tonne of material removed. This value is known to decrease with depth into the kimberlite pipe (Legrand 1980). At a certain point, it may be profitable to move to a second type of harvesting method, known as underground mining. This involves a similar process to the one described above, but rather than moving deeper into the Earth, small tunnels are cut into the earth horizontally. Smaller equipment is used to remove mined ore in underground situations. Some of this equipment can be operated by remote control. The research for this book began during a shift in production style from open-pit to underground methods. The move to underground mining was used by industry to renew local optimism by casting the transition as an opportunity for new sets of skills and, in turn, more high-wage work.

At the outset of my research, I attended industry conferences and read government materials on the mining sector. The message from national-level authorities echoed much of what I was used to hearing

---

3 For a discussion, see De Boeck's (2008) essay "Diamonds Without Borders: A Short History of Diamond Digging and Smuggling on the Border Between the Democratic Republic of Congo and Angola (1980–2008)" and other essays in Vlassenroot and Van Bockstael's (2008) *Artisanal Diamond Mining: Perspectives and Challenges*.

living in the NWT: there was a desperate need for primary sector workers. In 2005, the Mining Industry Training and Adjustment Council of Canada released *Prospecting the Future*, a 220-page study that proclaimed an urgent need for skilled workers to ensure Canada's ongoing competitiveness in the mining and minerals sector (MITAC 2005). The study estimated that 81,000 people would be needed to meet current and future industry needs. While state and academic discourse orients to notions of a growing knowledge economy, between 2002 and 2007, mining GDP growth was about twice the rate of the rest of the Canadian economy. Primary sector resource boom talk and labour shortage panic were transnational issues, as sparsely populated, resource rich states (Canada and Australia, in particular) tried to find ways to produce (affordable) workers for industry.

Given the optimistic labour market assessments and projections, I was surprised to learn that when diamond mines are in production, they require under 1,000 employees, over half of whom are considered to be "unskilled" or "semi-skilled." A large portion of employment opportunities come in the mine's construction and reclamation (closing) phases. Many of the open pits are at the bottom of drained lakes. Contract firms are hired to begin the process of draining and damming waterways to prepare for mineral extraction. Setting up the workers' camps and the processing facility are also a large part of the project.

Much of the labour process involved in Arctic industrial diamond mining is driving and maintaining heavy equipment. The other piece, which is often overlooked, is the work involved in reproducing labour. All three mine sites are remote. Workers stay on site for two-week rotations. This creates a significant amount of work in cleaning, cooking, and transporting workers around the site. I later learned that Trevor had actually already worked in the mines as a cook. The shifts were long and the pay not as high as he hoped. This new training course promised a much brighter future.

The speed with which mining companies hope to go from discovery into production means that the labour process to build and open a mine is divided in such a way that specialized teams are flown in for specific tasks. This way of preparing mines to open is much faster than local labour could ever be trained. As the mining companies in operation in the NWT are some of the world's largest, they have access to a substantial mobile labour pool that has taken local residents' place in the global production process, flying from site to site repeating the same limited sets of tasks. When I realized how relatively small the local workforce is for mining (800 jobs would be optimistic), I was honestly surprised. There seemed to be a mismatch between the level of economic promise and the actual prospect of long-term, stable employment for people like Trevor.

In many sectors of the economy – and in extractive industries, in particular – a company's merits are evaluated by consumers in terms of their reputation as "ethical." This has meant that many resource projects are now evaluated for their "social impacts and benefits" in addition to environmental monitoring. In northern Canada, CSR takes two concrete forms: impact benefit agreements (IBA) and socio-economic agreements (SEA). While these agreements are steeped in the language of the local, they are global industry standards for dealing with Indigenous populations. That there are two types of agreements is significant. The first type, IBAs, are signed with only the communities closest to the mines. These are confidential and can involve cash payouts and royalty sharing. The second type, SEAs, are made with the territorial government and are for the region as a whole. These are public, non-binding agreements that lay out how the project's social impacts will be assessed and set goals for hiring quotas and economic development initiatives.

As the NWT is ethnically diverse – nearly half of its population is non-Indigenous – the territorial government introduced SEAs to guarantee priority employment and business opportunities (tenders and subcontracts) to residents of the North (rather than, for example, attempting to institute a fair economic rent regime through a mining/resource tax, capital investment tax, or the creation of a heritage fund). SEAs helped to pave the way to diamond development by raising public support among non-Indigenous individuals. Citing employment and training as the supposed key benefits of contemporary resource projects, the SEAs were attractive to Northerners – as well as those in the process of formally becoming Northerners – as most are displaced working-class Canadians who have come north for work opportunities.

Some social science and journalist accounts tend to describe IBAs and SEAs as "viable approaches" in assuring Indigenous people will reap economic benefits from resource extraction (Gibson and Klinck

2005). Other analyses are more critical. The efficacy of IBAs in promoting social equality in the Canadian context is slowly being challenged. Myriam Laforce (2010) questions the ability of the IBA instruments to improve Indigenous participation in decision-making processes. Ken Caine and Naomi Krogman argue that power is unequally distributed among negotiating parties. Further, they argue that the confidentiality of IBAs can "stifle Aboriginal people from sharing information about benefits negotiated by other groups, prevent deeper understanding of long-term social impacts of development, thwart subsequent objections to the development and its impacts, and reduce visioning about the type and pace of development that is desirable" (Caine and Krogman 2010, 77). Because IBAs are confidential documents signed by the developer and the Indigenous authority, it is difficult to assess their terms (Sosa and Keenan 2001). In my experience, the secrecy of these agreements yields large-scale suspicion by those left out of knowing what is in them. The general assumption is they are extremely generous. My sense is that this is not the case. While existing criticisms are valuable, rarely do they note that these same processes have transformed much of the discussion around development from questions of Indigenous land and livelihood to questions of labour and work.

Over the course of my extended fieldwork in Canada's diamond basin, it was clear that the majority of Indigenous residents in the larger region do not directly experience the economic benefits of diamond development, even when projects happen on what are at various stages of becoming Indigenous title lands. For this reason, many Indigenous residents see development projects in terms very similar to non-Indigenous residents – that is, as a potential source for labour and employment. Education and work were repeatedly promoted as a benefit of mining not only by corporations, but by local people as well.

CONCLUSION

The corporate social responsibility initiatives that govern mining generally evaluate mines' effects on specific communities one at a time. Is *this* diamond mine good or bad for *this* group of people? These are ineffective questions. Communities have come into being alongside and against natural resource extraction over the last century (Golub

2014). This is what motivated me to move away from the singular focus on diamonds to the broader analysis of architectures of extraction. I move beyond the "is mining good or bad?" to investigate all that such questions imply. My choice to move away from the singular focus on diamonds to the broader analysis of architectures of extraction is my way of overcoming corporate social responsibility's reliance on, and reproduction of, a highly chronotopically constrained way of understanding culture and economy. A chronotope involves the construction of space and time in and through texts in such a way that is never unmediated or natural but always ideological and historically specific (Bakhtin 1981). This narrow view of extraction is what I am arguing makes Arctic issues that concern national publics (resource wealth, Indigenous poverty) harder rather than easier to understand. In looking at the ways in which people in the NWT enact different resource futures, we learn how CSR-style assessments are constrained along four intersecting axes.

The first constraint is *spatial*. Northern development schemes (notably natural resource development) presuppose that *natural resource extraction exclusively concerns the immediate population*. This forecloses the possibility of holding the local, national, regional, and global in the same analytic frame. Industrial mining relies on transnational formations of capital and labour. In fact, relations between existing populations and in-migrants are essential to understanding social organization in the area. Returning to the most recent socio-economic impact report, there is a focus on the "benefits" brought to what are called SLCs (small, local communities). These are the villages closest to the mines with an almost exclusively Indigenous population (usually under 500 people). These same sites have historically been the focus of anthropology, as more remote communities were thought to have better insight into "tradition." Multi-ethnic hubs like Hay River are often outside the area of assessment but are indeed critical elements in the architecture of extraction for both the physical and the human infrastructure they provide.

The second constraint is *temporal*. Diamonds-as-development presupposes that *individual resource projects are appropriate units of analysis* – or, said differently, individual mining companies are the most relevant targets of scrutiny. This forecloses a deep, contextually specific reading of the embeddedness of single projects in a much longer history of capitalist transformation in the area. It makes readings of Northern resource developments, as Piper (2009, 2) notes, "all too often historically blind," as if the North were "a blank canvas on which only current and future development will leave its mark." Great Slave Lake, otherwise known as "the diamond basin," is not unfamiliar with resource extraction. The Northwest Territories has the densest history of mineral extraction in North America. The list of natural resources that have left the Northwest Territories for global markets is long: fur (1800–1930), oil (1920–present), uranium (1930–50), gold (1930–2000), fish (1940–50), lead and zinc (1950–90), and now diamonds. The NWT is also a global destination of choice for exploration capital in the search for rare earths and oil/gas. Extractive industries have both displaced people and rooted them in place as the Canadian government created permanent settlements that pulled people away from life on the land. Given this long history of extraction, a single-commodity/community approach – which is very common in the social science of mining, particularly Arctic mining – would miss the essential elements in what makes new mining ventures move ahead.

The third analytic constraint is *racial/ethnic*. Northern development discourse presupposes that *Indigeneity is outside of history*, thus foreclosing an understanding of the making and unmaking of communities in relation to history and political economy. As Eric Wolf suggests, it is crucial to begin our enquiry by understanding "[local] communities as outcomes and determinants of historical processes; intimately connected with changes in the wider political and economic field" (Wolf 1986, 325). In the next chapter, I look at how the state configured ideas of Indigeneity in tandem with changing resource activities. These configurations managed to be both essential to and in the way of extraction.

The final constraint can be shorthanded as *aspirational*. When debating resource extraction, neither the concept of "curse" nor the concept of "cure" wholly captures the making of everyday life in the Northwest Territories. Some of my interlocutors certainly face challenges in their day-to-day efforts to get by. The connection between these difficulties and extractive industry are often not straightforward and often involve ambiguity and contradiction. What's more, extraction relies on local people's aspirations for the future – aspirations that are shaped, in part, by the long presence of industry and contemporary job training campaigns.

Through research and reflection, diamonds became less the focus of my study and more a prism through which I could see what I am calling the "architectures of extraction" that shape everyday life for people in the region. While the context for the book is the boom in Arctic diamonds, the next chapters move away from the luxury gemstone to the architectures that came before them. I illustrate how the necessary architectures of extraction in Canada's Arctic, as elsewhere, precede any single project, location, or ethnic community. This brings a wider set of social relationships into view and offers a rich portrait of the mechanics of extractive economies. The brief exchange in the jewellery store made clear to me what is so powerful and dangerous about ethical campaigns like the ones I have described in this chapter. They create a shorthand for complex problems and close out the possibility for curiosity and compassion.

DISCUSSION QUESTIONS

1 How do ethics play into your day-to-day consumption habits? Are there any brands/industries that you avoid for ethical reasons or that lead you to seek an "ethical alternative"? What about your preferred brand's marketing makes their claims believable? Are they simplifying anything to make themselves sound more attractive?

2 Describe some of the physical characteristics of diamonds. In what ways do those shape their social meanings?

3 The chapter outlines how "Canada" as brand does not have a stable meaning. What are some of the competing claims about Canada as they relate to diamond mining?

4 For the Love of God is a sculpture by artist Damien Hirst. It is a human skull encrusted with thousands of "non-conflict" diamonds. Find an image of the piece online. What kind of comment on society do you think the piece makes? Would you consider Hirst's piece ethical? Why or why not?

CHAPTER THREE

Race

If the expansion and consolidation of state power simply undermined, homogenized, and ultimately destroyed the distinctive societies and ethnic groups in its grasp, as various acculturation or melting pot theories would have it, the world would have long ago run out of its diverse ways of life, a supply presumably created at the dawn of time. To the contrary, state power must not only destroy but also generate cultural differentiation – and do so not only between different nation states, and between states and their political and economic colonies, but in the center of its grasp as well. The historical career of ethnic peoples can thus be understood in the context of forces that both give a people a birth and simultaneously seek to take their lives.

– *Gerald Sider (1987)*

My third night in my High Rise apartment, I was uneasy with myself. I was certain that I had overestimated the move into the building as the perfect jump-start to fieldwork. I lay awake lost in plans to improve as an ethnographer the next day when the distinctive thumping sound of hip-hop music started coming from the apartment next to mine. When I listened closely, I recognized the unmistakable sound of Flo Rida's club anthem from the early 2000s, "Low." It was three in the morning and the track was on repeat. I assumed the apartment next to mine was occupied by men who worked rotations in the diamond mines. Mine work typically consists of two weeks of twelve-hour shifts in the mines followed by two weeks out. One of the things I often heard was that men, especially those who were not married, went "overboard" with partying and spending money while not on shift (cf. Walsh 2003). I assumed the music I heard well into the early morning was part of the post-mine unwinding ritual.

The next morning, to my surprise, I saw a young woman come out onto the balcony next to mine. Her metal framed balcony door squeaked loudly. As did mine. Over time, this sound became the signal to the other that we wanted to talk. Even with the crisp October air, Destiny wore a slinky, lacy-strapped tank top and a zip-up hoody left undone. She had on dark sunglasses, the kind Audrey Hepburn might wear. Leaning on the iron railings and talking every evening until the snow made it impossible, I came to learn that Destiny was a twenty-two-year-old Dene woman, a hip-hop aficionado, an herbal tea lover, and an absolute perfectionist when it came to her appearance. She combined intricately braided hair with dark and glamorous eye makeup. She was a member of the K'atl'odeeche First Nation (reservation) across the river from the town of Hay River (see map 3.1). Destiny hadn't travelled far to move into the High Rise apartment next to mine yet she spoke like she was worlds away from her life on the reserve. "I'm never going back," she said, "Why would I want to be stuck over there?"

Even though the town and the First Nation are separated by a relatively narrow stretch of river, travel between the two isn't always straightforward. In winter, a ploughed ice road lets vehicles go across from reserve to town in under five minutes. The all-season bridge is at the town's southern boundary. In warmer weather, it takes about twenty-five minutes by car to make the fourteen-kilometre trip around and across, bumping along a dirt road. Taxi fare is $50 each way. In town, the First Nation is simply called "the reserve" and on the reserve, town is simply referred to as "across." Without vehicle access or sufficient resources, being "stuck on the reserve" can be taken literally.

"I got this apartment because I am going back to school," Destiny told me in our first balcony meeting. "I was just sick of all the partying and shit at my mom's. I just had it. With going to school I get my own place. I am gonna take real good care of it, like, keep it real clean and stuff." Determined to be an ideal tenant, Destiny would do a "killer clean" every Saturday before attending to her social plans for the

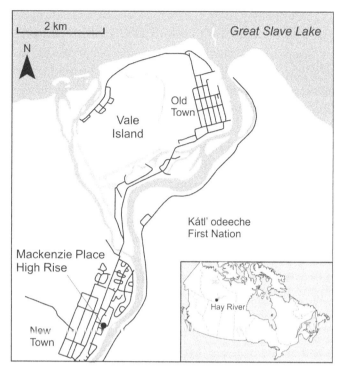

Map 3.1. Map of Hay River and K'atl'odeeche First Nation.
Source: ESRI Light Grey Canvas base map used with base map data provided from Esri, HERE, DeLorme, MapmyIndia, © OpenStreetMap contributors, and the GIS user community.

evening. Her apartment consistently smelled of bleach and hairspray. She decorated the walls with carefully lined photographs of family, friends, and eventually an anthropologist. She hung a poster of Tupac Shakur next to the Dene Nation flag.

"What are you taking at school?" I asked that first morning we met. She looked around as if the answer might be a dropped contact lens on the floor, "Um, like, mining, or something like that." As it turned out, Destiny was enrolled in a program I had been studying for several months. It was the same program Trevor was eagerly awaiting when I met him on my first day in the High Rise. Posters announcing jobs in underground mining were all over the Territories. While she may not have looked the part of a would-be miner, Destiny was precisely the kind of person mine development was said to help. She was a high school graduate living on sporadic wages earned cleaning or cooking in mineral exploration camps. At the time of my research, two of the NWT's diamond mines had exhausted open-pit sources and were supposed to move to underground harvesting to extend the mine's "lifecycle." This shift in production techniques was promoted as yet another opportunity for local labour, specifically Indigenous labour, to benefit from diamond mining. Destiny had enrolled in a state-industry training program for higher paid underground diamond mine work. She jumped on the offer when someone pointed it out to her. She let me know that it would be "real good money." Job training programs, like the one Destiny was enrolled in, are said to transform difficulties of everyday endurance into an opportunity to thrive by way of access to high-wage work associated with industry. In turn, diamonds from Canada's Arctic become ethical as they act as agents of regional development and personal transformation.

In my first exchanges with Destiny, it became clear that her housing and her hope for the future were attached to extractive industry in ways that my own weren't as a settler Canadian. This connection of Indigenous life to extractive capital is often taken for granted. Regardless of whether one believes that extraction is "good" for Indigenous communities or harmful, never is there an explanation of how categories of racial citizenship became so intertwined with extractive capital. Part of the larger aim in writing this book is to "make strange" these familiar political debates about Arctic futures, people, and landscapes. To do this, this chapter offers a historical and ethnographic account of racial architectures that enable extraction in Canada's Arctic. It chronicles the role of racial categories of personhood in the harnessing of diverse human energies to secure profits from the literal capture of nature in the Great Slave Lake basin. It does not offer a complete genealogy of place or a causal historical narrative. Instead, I focus on two people I came to know through chance encounters whose trajectories offer a window onto the dual history of the relationship between colonialism and capitalism in the region and beyond it. The first is Destiny. I came to understand how her life was enmeshed with resource extraction through our conversations as neighbours over the course of my year of fieldwork and through subsequent correspondence in the decade that followed. The second is John Hope, an employee of the Hudson's Bay Company who arrived in Hay River in the late 1800s and whom I came to know through archival documents.

I was able to contextualize Destiny's experience within the history of race and place by piecing together John Hope's movements in and out of the area. Initially, because of the very Anglo name, I assumed Hope was British. I came to learn of his complex and shifting Indigenous status through more archival digging. I first encountered John Hope as a name in an 1870 account book of the Hudson's Bay Company (HBC). The HBC was a fur-trading business for much of its existence and had imposed itself as the de facto government in parts of North America before European states and later the United States laid claim to some of those territories. The HBC was staffed by British transplants but relied on Indigenous people to capture fur-bearing animals. Hope was listed as one of eight waged employees. Adjacent to Hope and the other employees was a second list of names. These were "Indians" who received trade goods either for furs or for labour rendered (navigational assistance, providing meat and fish). At the top of the list was a "headman" by the name of "Britton," Destiny's family name.[1] I assumed that the layout of the account book reflected the organization of pre-national North America more generally, with Indigenous people listed in one column and settlers in the other. Through a process I describe in subsequent sections, I came to learn that Hope was Indigenous, although not local to the region. As I recount here, both Destiny and Hope are at once Indigenous and mobile, two terms often thought of as oppositional in the Canadian imaginary.

Taken together, Destiny and Hope conjure a "history of the present" (Roseberry 1989) that tracks the uneasy relationship between race/ethnicity, citizenship, and state-capital formation in the Northwest Territories. Their stories show how resource extraction in northern Canada simultaneously depends on and produces incommensurate forms of race, citizenship, locality, and mobility. As historical anthropologist Ann Laura Stoler (2010, 1, 4) writes, "colonial administrations

---

1 Given the relatively small population, I chose family pseudonyms which are uncommon to the area but which have similar qualities in terms of ethno-national origin. For example, here I use the family name "Britton" for Destiny. Like her own family name, this name is originally from Warwickshire, England, and was popular during the 1800s, when her family would have been given the name by traders. Most Anglophone names given to "Indians" in the region were usually Scottish (Norn) or Gaelic names, as the Hudson's Bay Company drew its workers from the Orkney Islands and the Scottish Highlands.

were prolific producers of social categories," and yet producing rules of classification was an unruly and piecemeal venture at best. She continues, "Archives are not simply accounts of actions or records of what people thought happened. They are records of uncertainty and doubt in how people imagined they could and might make the rubrics of rule correspond to a changing imperial world." This chapter is a historical narrative based in part on documents gathered in the colonial archives. It is necessarily partial and imperfect, as it relies on previous understandings that have been shaped by Western procedures and conventions, thus leaving out Indigenous perspectives on the past. Anthropologists have tried to grapple with the fact that the production of historical narratives involves the uneven contribution of competing groups and individuals who have unequal access to the means for such production (Trouillot 1995). To acknowledge these inequalities, I work "along the archival grain" (Stoler 2010) and focus less on a chronology of facts and more on the changing configurations of race, space, and citizenship over time and how that connected to resource extraction. What will become clear is that the approval of Arctic diamond mines is the culmination of longer struggles between Indigenous people, the colonial state, and resource industries and that race is the foundation for contemporary architectures of extraction.

HISTORICAL AND ECONOMIC BACKGROUND

Before moving into the story of Hope, it is necessary to understand a little more about the structure of the fur trade. For anthropologists, the mode of production in any given society is bound up with the cultural forms that uphold it. The fur trade began in eastern Canada in the mid-1600s and travelled westwards and northwards as sources were depleted. In 1670, the Crown awarded the Hudson's Bay Company exclusive commercial rights to the territory known as "Rupert's Land" via royal proclamation.[2] Capitalist development in the Great

---

2 Rupert's Land was a large parcel of land around Hudson Bay. Areas belonging to Rupert's Land were mostly in present-day Canada and included all of Manitoba, most of Saskatchewan, southern Alberta, southern Nunavut, and northern parts of Ontario and Quebec. It also included parts of Minnesota and North Dakota and very small parts of Montana and South Dakota (McIntosh and Smith 2006).

Slave Lake region does, by and large, begin with the fur trade. I was a little hesitant to begin this "history" section with the fur trade as it has become an "entrenched field of study in Canadian history, so universalizing that [it] appears to have been the [sole] preoccupation of Aboriginal as well as non-Aboriginal participants" (McCormack 2010, 25, drawing on Brown 1993). There is a long, important history before the fur trade; however, I start with it as I am interested here in what June Nash (1981) termed the "paradigm of integration of all people and cultures within a world *system*" (393, emphasis in original, as quoted in McCormack 2010, 25).[3]

The imperial fur trade was a form of merchant capitalism.[4] Merchant capitalism is defined by the purchase of commodities from communities that control and supervise their own production. Domination is at the point of exchange rather than the point of production. For fur traders, controlling labour without controlling production itself was not self-evident. Said another way, making sure Indigenous people trapped when and what traders wanted without overtly controlling them posed challenges to the HBC. Fur traders had to offer manufactured goods that were of interest to Indigenous trappers and at prices they deemed fair. If trappers felt they faced unfair terms of trade, they would travel elsewhere and trade with a competitor. Labour's mobility proved to be both essential to merchant capital (as they needed people to travel for furs) even as it threatened to undermine it (groups could trade at a rival post).

Another challenge to drawing local populations into capitalist production was that the main activities of domestic production,

---

3 The HBC-dominated fur trade was a form of original accumulation that facilitated capital growth by and for London's emerging securities market. Up to roughly 1800, this worked well for capitalists. Hudson's Bay Company Incorporated paid shareholders dividends of 60–70 per cent between 1690 and 1800. When the depression of 1857 hit, dividends fell below 10 per cent (Hudson's Bay Company 1866). With declining profits and new interests in industrial agriculture, the trade decreased in importance to British capitalists.

4 To these ends, I am relying loosely on the concept of "mode of production" as developed by Eric Wolf. For Wolf (1982), mode of production is not just a system of technology, nor a stage or type of society, but a heuristic tool used to focus on "strategic" relationships of power and wealth. It includes the social, not merely the economic. The inclusive term "social reproduction" includes the reproduction of the relations and social institutions necessary to sustain capitalism.

specifically caribou hunting and fishing, were in many ways at odds with fur production, as locations of these raw materials were all different. For example, prior to the fur trade, the people of the Great Slave Lake and Peace River regions had a use-oriented or domestic mode of production. The primary goal of production was family survival (Asch 1979, 1977; McCormack 2010). In brief, small kin groups or bands (roughly twenty-five to fifty people) produced goods for their own use. These groups were broadly egalitarian, with primary divisions of work being based on age and, to a much lesser extent, gender. Local bands would be tied together into regional bands in order to maintain social and political connections that afforded safety in times of resource scarcity (Helm 1968). The area where the Hay River meets Great Slave Lake provided ample fishing opportunities for domestic production that later articulated with capitalist production. It was a winter gathering site for multiple local bands. According to anthropologist June Helm (1968), this regional group that came together was not at the outset politically cohesive, but through intensification of the fur trade would become so in the 1900s. Fur traders increasingly tried to convert populations away from subsistence activities by advancing food, guns, ammunition, traps, cloth, blankets, liquor, and tobacco. Items that could facilitate domestic production (e.g., fish nets, twine for net-making) were restricted from trade. Advances of food staples such as flour, lard, and tea led to a decline in the autonomous hunting activities of the trapping population. A consistent interest in producing furs by trappers was not guaranteed. Trade officials often described local populations as "lazy." I understand this as a testament to the inability to fully harness productive labour. For example, at Hay River, fishing provided a strong subsistence base. In the journals of HBC traders, this was cause for many complaints about the "Indians" being content to "just" fish. A trading post at Hay River opened and closed multiple times, owing to the difficulties in harnessing human energies for merchant capital and the fur trade.

Trading posts necessarily became spaces laden with social bonds that could draw labour back on a consistent basis. This was achieved in part by the advancement of credit in the form of goods, or foodstuffs in the event of a particular season of scarcity. It was also achieved by giving gifts or advances to "chiefs" or "head traders." This practice favoured smaller bands and led to new forms of power within groups. Merchant capital can, and did, encourage the emergence of leaders and domination within production (Sider 2003a). This detail will become significant when we look at the institutionalization of Indian "bands" vis-à-vis the state in 1899/1900. Ethnic difference was another piece that was central to organizing the labour process. Perceived differences between groups helped fur trade officials establish where to set up a trading post and build alliances that would ensure the return of trappers to particular locales that had given them advances. While there was a general sense that all Indians could be willing trappers, there was a lot of work done on the part of trade officials to identify ethnic groups (e.g., Slavey, Beaver, Cree). In fact, it would not be until the onset of Canadian state making that the diversity of different groups would be subsumed under the label "Indian." For traders, knowing existing social relations and conflicts allowed them to build alliances and restrict mobility of trade (e.g., allowing only certain ethnic groups to trade at particular posts) and ultimately helped to keep costs down and minimize resistance from labour (Krech 1984).

It is worth noting that when direct trade began in the subarctic region between 1820 and 1870, the shift from domestic production to increased capitalist production was not a foregone conclusion. When traders arrived, the assumption was that all "Indians" were trappers. The labour process of fur trapping needed "Indians" to do certain tasks and those tasks were in turn Indianized. While the bands in the region were skilled hunters and gatherers, the materials sought after by capital were not the ones they had used in great quantity in domestic forms of production. Local populations possessed the kinds of knowledge and skills adaptable to this type of labour. However, they did not necessarily want to or have to participate, particularly not on terms they did not deem beneficial. As Wolf (1982, 161) explains, the fur trade "deranged [sic] accustomed social relations and cultural habits, it prompted the formation of new responses – both internally, in the daily life of human populations, and externally in relations among them…. It led to the decimation of whole populations and the displacement of others to new habitats." Importantly, "many of the Indian 'nations' or 'tribes' later recognized as distinct ethnic identities by government agents or by anthropologists took shape in response to the spread of the fur trade itself, a process which the native Americans were as much active participants as the traders, missionaries, or soldiers of the encroaching Europeans" (Wolf 1982, 194). Fur trade–era politics are essential components in the contemporary architectures of extraction that guide contemporary mining practice.

AN ARCHIVAL ACCIDENT

I first encountered the name John Hope in the back of a former Hudson's Bay Company store turned local museum in Hay River in 2009. Like all the houses in the "old town," the long wooden building was propped up on concrete legs to avoid flood damage should the water levels rise. Painted white with a red trim, the museum had been a hard-won project put together by a few non-Indigenous volunteers. The building is unheated and only open for a few months in the summer. I went to the museum because Catherine, one of the museum's founders, welcomed me to dig through their materials. In the diary of the 1870 postmaster, I read a rather cross reporting that Hope and another man were responsible for a fire on New Year's Eve. The fire destroyed one of two buildings at the fledgling Hay River post. I found myself imagining a small wooden building in flames. I could hear the crackling sounds ringing through the January night air. Temperatures are usually -40°C at that time of year. The stillness of extreme cold is the most vivid memory I have of living in the high Arctic years ago. It brings a haunting feeling, a reminder of how vulnerable you are in relation to matters of weather and isolation. Soon after, I found the 1870 account book where Hope was listed as one of eight waged employees. I could see from cross-referencing other account books that Hope had to use his earnings to replace what he lost in the fire, essentially making him an indentured servant. Hope's occupation was listed as "interpreter." Paid bilingualism among HBC employees was out of the ordinary and now Hope had earned my full attention. Translation was usually left to men of the church or to Indigenous traders. Although the region is considered Dene (Athabascan) territory, in general, Cree, Chipewyan, English, and French were the dominant languages of trade (McCormack 2010). I initially left the matter of Hope aside and continued to take notes on other materials, but his name coupled with the story of the fire and my interest in linguistic difference in the colonial era meant that he would stir my imagination often.

I decided to travel to the Hudson's Bay official archives in Winnipeg, Manitoba. There I pieced together Hope's path to and from Hay River and found his movements revealing of the complicated ways in which race and political economy articulated between roughly 1825 and 1900.

I was surprised to learn that John Hope was baptized an "Indian boy" by Reverend J. West at the Red River settlement in 1825 (Hudson's Bay Company 2002). I had, until then, assumed he was not Indigenous. While the HBC had been in pursuit of fur since roughly 1670, by the time Hope was born, its monopoly on the trade was in jeopardy. Fur sources were depleting in and around Hudson Bay. The company's desire to move inland in search of more furs and to cut off rival traders placed new demands on the company's labour. The HBC had difficulty convincing their existing post staff to move away from the single-season work around the bay that had characterized the industry up until that point and to instead take lengthier, more dangerous contracts that involved travel to the northwest (Burley 1997). The response around the 1820s was to hire "Canadian" labour, which, given that the Canadian state did not yet exist, largely meant the descendants of French settlers or Métis trappers who had worked for the rival Northwest Company, which merged with the HBC in 1821.

In part of the region that is now Manitoba, the Red River settlement was a colonization project started in 1811 after many Scottish people were made destitute through the Highland enclosures. Thomas Douglas, Fifth Earl of Selkirk, established the colony for landless Scots. The HBC, which had acquired the land through imperial seizure, sold the tract to Selkirk for two reasons. First, it was a way to have local agricultural development that could feed its workers; second, parcels of land could be offered to its labourers upon retirement. This was an incentive strategy meant to deal with the difficulty the HBC had in attracting and retaining workers for the trading posts. Beyond the much-needed "Indian" trappers, the process demanded transportation, infrastructure building and maintenance, food production, trading, and accounting. As Burley (1997) explains, the strategy of providing land as an incentive backfired, as many men took their plots early and refused to return to work. Red River was never a wide-open empty space. Rather, it was an area that had long been occupied by trappers working for HBC's rival, The Northwest Company. Their armed resistance to Selkirk's presence laid the foundation for the collective identity known as Métis, which remains an important part of the Canadian political-legal fabric today.

As a child, Hope showed great promise in his ability to read and write in English. Reverend West selected Hope and three other boys to become missionaries to their own people. Much disliked by the HBC officials and retirees, who felt that West spent too much time "doting on the Indians," the Reverend was dismissed after two years of service (J.S. Scott 2005). The other two prodigies were given their own missions before West returned to England. Young Hope eventually joined the Hudson's Bay Company as an "honorable servant" in the parlance of the time (HBC 2002). Hope was hired in 1863 to help paddle large canoes Northwest into the Mackenzie District. By 1868, Hope had arrived on the south shore of Great Slave Lake. He helped to establish the Hay River fort (roughly the same place where Destiny and I will turn up 140 years later).

While Hope was busy helping to navigate and change the local landscape, important political economic changes were underway, both near and far. First, the Crown sold the HBC to a group of British financiers whose priorities would shift and split from furs to industrial development. Canadian confederation occurred in 1867, but the nascent nation-state would not acquire the land where Hope was (the Northwestern Territory) until the Hudson's Bay Company sold it to Canada in 1870. Envious and fearful of the United States' rising industrial production, together the new Dominion and British finance capital worked together to expand Canada from east to west, drawing western resources eastwards for the expansion of industrial centres based in Ontario and Quebec.

The far Northwest was not part of the national project during the early years of confederation. The focus was on agricultural development, which was thought to be ill-suited to northern soils and temperatures. As such, the region above the "fertile belt" (roughly the 200 kilometres north of the US border) was seen as undevelopable, and Northern populations were said to be "better left as Indians" (Coates 1993). Throughout Hope's years of service, the new Canadian state remained disinterested in fully incorporating the northern regions into its political and economic landscape. It sought to avoid the high costs (notably in the form of infrastructure for health and education) of extending citizenship rights northwards, and therefore support for the reproduction of Northern populations was left largely to the church and remaining trade activity.

With declining interest in furs, the Hay River fort closed in 1873 and Hope was promoted to postmaster at nearby Fort Rae (Behchokǫ̀). That same year marked the beginning of "the long depression," the first international financial crisis, which ended Britain's exclusive claims to industrial dominance. In efforts to recapture some of the imperial power's losses, expedited plans for development in new and former colonies began. In Canada, this primarily meant rail development through the borrowing of British capital. Across midwestern Canada, there was the outstanding issue of unconverted Indigenous populations who were without the economic base that had sustained them (fur and game) and who were increasingly either dying or causing civil "unrest," both of which challenged the legitimacy of the new state (Kalant 2004; Kulchyski 2005, 2007).

The post-confederation Numbered Treaty system (1871–1921) was meant to address both issues (see map 3.2). Numbered treaties were used by the Canadian state to serially extinguish significant (though not all) Indigenous claims to land title in exchange for economic and social support from the federal government, essentially swapping claims (and often use of land/resources) for quasi-incorporation into the Canadian nation-state and a modicum of political and legal standing. Treaties ceded Indigenous title to land and significant subsoil rights in exchange for recurring payments and welfare provisions of education and health services/care to Indigenous residents in the region (Coates and Morrison, 1986a, 1986b; Fumoleau 2004). The eleven treaties cover most of central and northwestern Canada. Each includes different terms, as we will see. Some provided farming tools to heads of kin groups, others (in the case of the Northern Treaties 8 and 11) included guarantees of hunting and fishing rights. While Hope moved from post to post in the Mackenzie District between 1871 and 1877, the political landscape to the south changed significantly, with Treaties 1–7 settling lands covering much of what are Ontario, Manitoba, Saskatchewan, and southern Alberta.

Hope married a woman described in the census as "Indian" from Fort Simpson and together they had a son. When Hope retired from the company in 1883, he headed south to the newly formed province of Saskatchewan. He returned to the Church of England that had

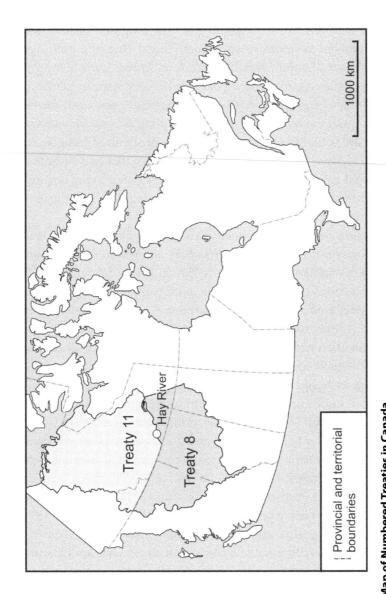

Map 3.2. Map of Numbered Treaties in Canada.

Source: ESRI Light Grey Canvas base map used with base map data provided from DLI (2012), Esri, HERE, DeLorme, MapmyIndia, © OpenStreetMap contributors, and the GIS user community.

schooled him long ago. In his final years, he served as a Sunday school teacher at the newly instituted vocational residential school for Indians in Battleford. His knowledge of Cree and his allegiance to the Church made him an asset to the first state-initiated venture into Indian education: residential vocational training. While much has been written on residential schooling in Canada, few have remarked that the earliest ventures were specifically vocational schools organized around anticipated national economic priorities. In this way, we see a thread between Hope and Destiny's participation in a mine training program.

BETWEEN HOPE AND DESTINY

Hope's status as a Christian evaded the term "Indian" in reports written about his service. In the notebooks of his superiors and colleagues he was never racialized. My discovery of his shifting status only came with the location of his birth record and later from census data of 1881; both labelled him "Indian," the former by birth, the latter as "nationality." These shifting categories are essential components in the architecture of extraction. This will become clear as I bridge the historical gap between Hope and Destiny.

After Hope's departure, the old HBC post building was taken up by an "Indian chief" who had been encouraged by the Roman Catholic Church to settle in the area. A year later, in 1893, at the request of the chief, an Anglican mission was established. Free traders from central Canada and the United States began to set up small posts in the region in attempts to compete with the HBC. Encouraging competing churches and trading posts to settle in the same area was a way for local Indigenous trappers to secure better terms of trade and more consistent access to goods, which made trapping and fishing easier.

As the twentieth century approached, population changes would bring social and economic shifts. Prior to 1900, Hay River consisted of two small missions and several extended Slavey kin groups. The total population never exceeded eighty persons, of which five to ten were church officials and traders, while the remaining seventy were Slavey groups whose encampments were at the mouth of the river, where fish were abundant (Zarchikoff 1975). Within the Anglican Church, there were a number of "Native helpers." These were converted Indigenous individuals from the neighbouring communities of Fort Resolution or Fort Chipewyan where direct trade and missions began much earlier. Intermarriage between male "Native helpers" and female "Indians" was common, as was marriage between non-Indigenous churchmen and female "Native helpers." Native helpers were often translators and eventually missionaries in their own right.

The turn of the twentieth century brought gold and mineral rushes, and prospectors began passing through the Hay River fort on their way to stake their claims. The mission's guest book of 1898 lists 120 visitors in a single summer season. It was after the rise in "visitors" that Anglican Reverend T.J. Marsh noted that the Indians at Hay River began to take an interest in learning English, saying "the Indians now began to think it would be a good thing to learn English and were as eager to learn as they were backward before" (*Historical Sketch* 2012).

In the initial years of the mission, Marsh had noted that "the Indians demanded exorbitant wages for their labour" (*Historical Sketch* 2012). However, their demands dropped after passersby who were stuck due to weather often exchanged labour for food and shelter. While I cannot be sure, it would seem from the early mission's reports that local populations did not see their labour power as a commodity. In his diary, Reverend Marsh remarked that often the "Indians" would take pity on him and offer him fish and refuse payment. Fish, at least at this time, was thought of more as a gift than it was as a commodity. This would change when a local/regional market for fish would emerge.

Cultivating Christians and citizens in colonial Canada, like elsewhere, produced oddly mixed results. From the Hay River mission diary, it was observed that converting the Indians at Hay River was a challenge and that they would only engage with their Christian neighbours on their terms. One missionary in 1894 remarked, "If she showed them pictures or told them a story they would listen, but if she began to talk to them of sin they would tell her they never sinned. They seemed to have no feeling of need for a Saviour. It seemed like trying to break down a thick stone wall with a few pebbles. They could make no impression as far as spiritual things were concerned, though the Indians improved in other ways" (*Historical Sketch* 2012, 14).

Throughout the long depression of 1873–96, church missions in sparsely populated places like the Canadian North received smaller amounts of financial support from their parent institutions. The mission school that was established at Hay River opened with seven students from neighbouring posts in 1895. The Indigenous groups around Hay River largely ignored schooling. Pupils for the school were, instead, drawn from converted families around the region, notably the communities farther east and south that had had longer direct contact with missionaries. With barely enough food to feed the boarding pupils, Marsh regularly received fish from the Indians, who found his attempts to be self-sufficient through gardening to be futile (*Historical Sketch* 2012). The school could not expand until it received further financial support from the state, as church sources were few. It is under these conditions that we can understand why the church would be involved in facilitating the Numbered Treaty process that would eventually help to create the reserve that Destiny was so keen to leave.

While groups in the Great Slave Lake basin actively resisted the treaties initially, particularly their use of reservations, they began to consider them if they could bring in resources and protect hunting and fishing rights in the face of growing numbers of prospectors and competing commercial fishermen from other parts of Canada. The northern regions were not agriculturally valuable to the state, so they set up northern treaties without reservations, although the agreements contained the possibility for them later. Despite treaty promises to protect hunting and fishing rights, there was increased competition over these resources by non-Indigenous people. Those who were now "Treaty Indians" increasingly protested and refused to accept the annual payments of $5.[5]

While the state ignored early protests regarding the terms of Treaties 8 and 11, the formation of the political movement of the Indian Brotherhood of the 1970s (based on the civil rights–style movements in the United States and influenced by Québécois nationalism in Canada), coupled with the possibility of a northern oil pipeline running

---

5 This is the equivalent of about C$150 in 2021 currency; however, the payment remains C$5 to this day.

through the Territory, meant that the state reached a discursive impasse. Its national history (colonialism, dispossession) was now a challenge to its social and economic future (cf. Povinelli 2002, 18). The ethnic division between Indian groups and Métis was now a point for political mobilization in the interest of reclaiming land rights. The Brotherhood (later renamed the Dene Nation) rejected the categories of Métis, non-status, and Treaty Indian – which were argued to be imposed categories meant to impede solidarity. In July 1975, the Dene Nation passed the Dene Declaration, which at once affirmed solidarity across these groups and their right to self-determination (Erasmus 1977).

Despite important regional solidarities between Indigenous people, kin groups around the Hay River needed more urgent strategies. In the 1970s, the town of Hay River announced that it would be relocating a few last "Treaty Indians" away from the east bank to new housing on the west side of the settlement. The existing area consisted of a small wooden Catholic church and graveyard. The plan was to cover the area in four feet of gravel to make a marshalling yard for a proposed pipeline project. Going back to the terms of Treaty 8, an emergent Indigenous political group sought legal help through the federal Department of Indian Affairs to lobby for a reservation that would obstruct this plan. Power derives, in part, from the ability to turn space into place (Harvey 1989). At first blush, the existence of a reservation might signal the marginalization of an ethnic group. Indeed, across the United States and Canada, the systematic seizure of lands and relocation of Indigenous populations to reservations throughout 1850s to the 1930s accomplished precisely that. In the case of the Northwest Territories, the story is much more complicated. It was part of a struggle to define how local place would be positioned in the context of a "modernizing" town. Hay River's contemporary geography of difference is part of a longer transformation process.

The K'atl'odeeche First Nation became the only reservation in the Northwest Territories. It formed in 1975, only a year after the construction of the High Rise, where Destiny and I now lived. Bertie Britton, Destiny's grandfather, was elected chief in the late 1970s. He was part of the political organization that brought the Hay River reserve into being. As mining activity in the region increased, Bertie and others saw a reservation as a way to respect the past and carve a future for their people. The reservation was a political project whose social and economic preconditions can be traced to the mid-1800s, described above. In many ways, this reinforced the boundary between Treaty Indians and others. The reserve was enabled by federal Indian policy from the 1930s – a place of recognition – but left many Indigenous people living on the other side of the river and outside of the process.[6]

During the same period, the Dene Nation was successful in bringing Indigenous social and economic inequalities to the forefront of the Canadian imagination. Throughout the 1970s and early 1980s, Dene Nation leader George Erasmus continued to underscore the danger of fragmenting policies and lobbying the state on behalf of the larger region. The group was able to place pipeline development on hold for ten years, in order to allow for new land claim agreements to be settled. In 1978, Métis and Dene representatives rejected the land claims proposal suggested by the state. At this point, funding for negotiations between the people of the NWT was suspended. The challenge of solidarity across 70,000 square kilometres now aggravated, the Dene Nation struggled to try to adequately represent the full region. After another rejected proposal, the federal government proclaimed that they would no longer negotiate with the entire Dene Nation; they would only be negotiating regionally with smaller groups. Internal divisions within the Dene Nation grew increasingly acute. Their neighbours to the north, the Inuvialuit (who had never been included in the Numbered Treaty system), had reached a settlement in 1984. The newly formed Inuvialuit Regional Corporation and its shareholders began to receive dividend payments from oil and gas explorations.

By 1993, the fragments began to break away, with the groups whose unsettled claim areas stretched along the Mackenzie Valley gas corridor withdrawing from the Dene Nation. The shift to regional representation unsettled the politics of Indigeneity and regional solidarities – at once according more autonomy to Indigenous groups while at the same time politicizing their respective differences with one another. These processes made land claims dependent on and exacerbated differences between groups, many of whom had up to that

---

6 A smaller First Nation was established in 1993 in West Channel. These are people who were descendants of fishing families who had not taken treaty.

point identified more closely with a local community than with a linguistic or cultural nation. Likewise, the economic stakes of large-scale resource allocations drove wedges within groups according to the sorts of internal inequalities that had long beset Indigenous peoples (see also Dombrowski 2008).

DESTINY TAKES OFF

When I started teaching in the most northernly district of the NWT, I had been warned that there was "high transience" between Northern communities. I was told that students and parents would simply "take off." It was sometimes implied by teachers that it was a failure on the part of parents to "get it together." From Destiny, I started to learn how "taking off' is just the opposite; it is a way of getting it together. Over the course of eighteen months of fieldwork straddling the rise and decline of Canada's diamond industry (2007–9), Destiny would tell me about the many times she had "taken off." Sitting on the worn tweed sofa of my rental apartment, sipping tea, she used scars and knife wounds to narrate her life, weaving physical traces of harm (as bar brawls, dog bites, or domestic assault) into stories of family, community, love, and betrayal. Sometimes she took off to see kin on a reservation south of her own, other times she went in search of work in one of the many exploration camps that dot this region. Other times, she would be looking for a new romantic interest, lamenting there were "no good men around here." The matter-of-fact tone she used to describe her injuries made clear that stories of her difficulties were not meant to solicit my sympathies. "I'm a Dene woman. I can handle my shit," she'd remind me.

The first time Destiny "took off," she was fifteen years old. Her grandfather, Bertie, had died the week before. Bertie was the primary caregiver in their extended family and raised Destiny in what she called "the Dene way." He lay in the hospital for two weeks before he passed away. The hospital is "across" while Destiny lived on the reserve at the time. Destiny visited with her grandfather almost every day she could "catch a ride" from the reserve to the hospital in town. She and Bertie would spend their visits teasing each other in the way they always had.

One day Destiny arrived at the hospital to find that her grandfather's bed was no longer in the room where she had spent countless hours visiting him. She ran up and down the three small hallways of the community hospital screaming, "Where the fuck is he?" until one of the nurses grabbed her, looked at her apologetically and showed her to his body. The day her grandfather died, Destiny had spent over an hour trying to catch a ride "across." Years after Bertie's political actions to create a reserve, the very space he had created for his community would be the space that Destiny could not cross quickly enough to see him before his death. His own political efforts enmeshed in larger structures that continue to restrict who moves freely in this region and how they do so.

"A week after Grandpa died," Destiny explained, "my cousin said, 'Let's fuckin' take off' And I was like, 'Yeah, what's the point of staying around here?'" Destiny and her cousin hitchhiked from Hay River southbound along the Mackenzie Highway to the reservation at Meander River, Alberta. The Mackenzie Highway was the first road that connected "north" with "south." It begins in Grimshaw, Alberta, and runs 600 kilometres to Hay River. Before it was a road, it was a tractor trail, before it was a tractor trail it was the route Indigenous trappers took to trade at Fort Vermillion when there were no posts at Hay River, or their prices/goods were deemed insufficient.

Destiny's earliest account of "taking off" reveals the edges of a chronotopically constrained vision of Indigenous well-being proposed by state-industry and often mobilized by communities. As described in chapter 2, the "social licence to operate" mines in the NWT (and in many other parts of the world) is achieved through political-legal mechanisms (impact benefit agreements, socio-economic agreements) that are organized between single communities and single projects. Yet Bertie's efforts and Destiny's ability to live with their outcomes reveal that resource struggles and the architecture of extraction exceed any one project. Contemporary efforts vis-à-vis mining can only be understood against the backdrop of changing assemblages of race, capital, and nature in this region. Destiny's engagements with diamond mining today are linked to her grandfather's efforts to curb an oil pipeline in the past. The conditions that enabled Bertie and other Dene people to use the reservation system as defence on the encroachment of Dene spaces of/for life thwarted Destiny's efforts to see her grandfather alive one last time and pushed her to "take off" for the first time.

Destiny's return to her hometown came after a significant injury. "This," she said, as she pointed to a jagged scar that ran almost the full length of her calf, "was from some crazy fucking dog, when I took off to the Wandering Reserve, after Grandpa died. I was just minding my own business waiting for my man. Then, this dog breaks off its chain and friggin' attacks me. I had to get medi-evacced to Edmonton."

In Northern communities, medical resources are limited to nursing stations. Anything requiring advanced and urgent intervention leads to "medical evacuation" by airplane to a hospital in Edmonton. Destiny explained the procedure as "lots of surgeries taking skin from my ass and putting it on my face." She rolled down the right leg of her stretch pants and pointed to two small white scars on her cheek. What stood out to her in recalling her time in hospital was not the pain associated with multiple skin grafts. "The band paid for my whole family to come and be there with me. My whole family. They were there."

Bertie, Destiny's grandfather, along with other leaders of that era, made moves to create a reservation, and this caused some tension between the larger Indigenous leadership. Some saw it as undermining the collective process of moving forward to a larger land claim. Yet it would later afford this group some autonomy to, when circumstances arise, fund far-reaching care, as was the case with Destiny's hospital stay after the dog bite. The financial capacity to bring Destiny's family down to the hospital was an ability she nor her family had on their own accord and thus it was significant to her. Being deemed worthy of her band's collective purse gave her a sense of pride that she was cared for and indeed a member of a community. Destiny's sentiments of ethnic attachment wax and wane. It is precisely her experience of harm, and her community's ability to respond ethically to it, that shored up a sense of belonging, even if fragile.

CONCLUSION

On several scales, mining depends on the movement of labour into and out of development regions to ensure forms of social regulation and economic productivity commensurate with global industry's imperatives. Destiny and Hope show us that while capital is adept at harnessing expended populations to these ends, it cannot single-handedly produce them. In addition to demand for unequally divided labour, capitalist expansion depends on establishing and maintaining sovereignty over areas to access raw resources. Establishing sovereignty and dividing labour pose a dialectical challenge to state and capital. The social process of differentiation aims to meet this dual challenge. The history between Hope and Destiny is meant to elaborate how citizenships and locality, as means of differentiation, are the architectures of extraction used by state, capital, and social actors in different, and partially incompatible, ways. As a result, tensions arise, underlining a core contradiction of liberal citizenship, namely unequal inclusion.

What is at stake is the relationship between enclosure and differentiation. Differentiation occurs at the nexus of economic imperatives, state power, and existing differences (Cooper and Stoler 1997; Sider and Smith 1997). Differentiated citizenships (differential positionings in relation to rights, benefits, protections; see Sider 2003b) are a crucial feature of modern states for legitimizing unequal divisions of labour/resources, yet they cannot be fully managed or produced by the state itself. Differentiated citizenships and inequalities that come to be named race or gender, for example, become harnessable vulnerabilities that simultaneously "produce, or deeply participate in the production of enduring inequalities" while allowing the state to claim that it has one set of rules that apply to all (Sider 2003b, xv).

Racial categories of personhood, and struggles to work within and against them, are essential components of the architecture of extraction in Canada's Arctic. John Hope's baptized name signals that the system is driven by law (in conjunction with the contingencies of capitalist political economy) on the one side and his own hope and mobility on the other. The changes, which situate Destiny and John Hope within and against categories of Indigeneity, reveal how, in the first instance, states reproduce locality to maintain sovereignty and make resources available to capital. At the same time, however, to harvest those same resources and reproduce locality and labour at a cost attractive to state and capital, populations are circulated to and from frontier zones of extraction. This leads these populations to increase local competition over resources, which drives wages down and the cost of living up. The contradiction is that existing local populations need to increasingly rely on the state for social reproduction. What sustains the working side of the equation is not status or cultural difference, as Destiny's story points out – they are far too ambivalent and tainted concepts; rather, it is hope that achieves this work.

DISCUSSION QUESTIONS

1 In what ways does resource extraction depend on race in northern Canada?

2 Reflect on the quote by Gerald Sider (2006, xv): "Differentiated citizenships and inequalities that come to be named race, or gender (for example) become harnessable vulnerabilities that simultaneously produce, or deeply participate in the production of enduring inequalities while allowing the state to claim that it has one set of rules that apply to all." What do you understand this to mean? Can you think of an example that would illustrate this claim?

3 How did political strategies used by Indigenous people in one generation come to support and/or impede their goals in subsequent generations?

4 Archives house historical documents that shed light on the past. They are also cultural institutions. In your opinion, in what ways are archives "cultural"?

CHAPTER FOUR

Infrastructure

Two structures mark the centre of the subarctic transportation town of Hay River. The first is an eight-foot inuksuk. The second is the "tallest residential building" in the Territory, the Mackenzie Place High Rise. When the High Rise was built in the 1970s, it was the centrepiece of a "new town" that could host resource-rich futures imagined to be on the horizon. It was to be a beacon of modernity on the edge of Canada's Arctic. Across the street from the High Rise, the inuksuk stands on the lawn of the fire station and town hall. Inuksuit are stone cairns once used as navigational markers on Arctic landscapes that otherwise held few distinctive features. While inuksuit are typically built from found stones, this one is an imitation made of a tan resin and is hollow inside. Inuksuit often symbolize permanent connection to place, landscape intimacy, and reference Canada's northernmost ethno-cultural group: Inuit.

The High Rise and the inuksuk present themselves as distinct symbols with separate semiotic duties. They each point to configurations of time and space outside of the present. The inuksuk points to a distant past, while the High Rise was intended to mark the way to a "modern" future. Simultaneously "modern-in-the-making" and "ethnically traditional," Hay River, like much of the Canadian North, is often talked about in terms of these temporal polarities, always reaching out and away to some other time, never fully being a kind of acceptable present. Despite their differences, both structures were

erected in the latter half of the 1970s, the previous resource boom decade for the region before diamonds. Their competing ideas of what
constitutes northern Canada forms the basis of the next element in the
architecture of extraction: infrastructure.

Anthropologists Anand, Gupta, and Appel (2018, 3, 4) argue that
"material infrastructures, including roads and water pipes, electricity
lines and ports, oil pipelines and sewage systems, are dense social,
material, aesthetic, and political formations that are critical both to
differentiated experiences of everyday life and to expectations about
the future." They ask, "what do infrastructures promise? What do
infrastructures do? And what does attention to their lives – their
construction, their use, maintenance and breakdown; their poetics,
aesthetics, and form – reveal?" In this chapter, I attend to the life of
the High Rise from its earliest beginnings to today to show how the
natural resource present is shaped by experiences with infrastructures from the past. I argue that the shortcomings of resource-driven
"modernization" efforts in Canada's Arctic do not only undermine
extractive processes but enliven them as well.

This chapter describes the physical and semiotic trajectory of the
High Rise chronologically. First, the section "Promises" outlines the
motivations for the building as the centrepiece of the town's modern
redevelopment after a flood in the 1960s and in the midst of a heated
debate about a potential oil and gas pipeline through the region.
I pay attention to the future-oriented promises this type of development made in this community and across the Arctic more broadly.
The second section, "Divergences," tracks the immediate debates over
the building and how these signalled multiple, competing visions for
the region's future. I show how infrastructure became a resource in
its own right. With few local people able to engage in costly mining
ventures, local elites competed over construction contracts for building infrastructure to support extractive development. The exclusion
of most Indigenous people from this "infrastructural prospecting"
paved the way for contemporary corporate social responsibility
agreements. The third section, "Disappointments," focuses on the
last decades, since the building has fallen into increased disrepair. For
many local people, it represents problems attributed to frontier economies: poverty, transience, addiction, and crime. The chapter describes
tenants' and non-tenants' laments about the structure to track what

Greenberg (2014) calls the "social life of disappointment." I show how disappointments with existing resource-driven infrastructure animate contemporary mining debates. In the conclusion, I return to the in-uksuk, who, much like the High Rise, has been subject to changing and contested meanings. Such debates over the meaning of Northern infrastructure are instructive of how people try to shape their relationship to the region's past, present, and future. Taken together, the chapter works to show how the material finitude and hubris that is inherent in both infrastructure and extractive industry still somehow look to the future. This forward-looking impulse, even in the face of a building's decay, helps make sense of how diamond development was embraced rather eagerly.

PROMISES

The presence of a lone high-rise tower on a subarctic landscape is striking and impossible for any visitor to ignore. High-rise residential towers like this one were increasingly common in the postwar northeastern United States after World War II. Inspired by Swiss-French architect Le Corbusier's "radiant city" concepts from the 1930s, tall, high-density housing was a hallmark of Western architectural modernity in big cities. The new building would be able to house well over 300 people and offered amenities like a coin laundromat and convenience store, accessible from within the building. The original drawings included a second-story, aboveground tunnel to the businesses across the street. This type of modern architectural feature became a staple in cold Canadian cities trying to solve the issue of confronting winter weather. The High Rise was officially named Alexander Mackenzie Place, after the Scottish explorer credited with mapping many northern regions and waterways (see figure 4.1). Like many things in settler colonial Canada, these naming practices were integral in erasing Indigenous presence and imagining places as white.

In this small community, the High Rise looks desperately out of place. It is rare to see a tower of this scale not beside others. Unlike most high-rise towers, which face other towers, this one casts its midnight summer shadow on what feels like an endless stretch of taiga. With Hay River's community population of 4,000, the building seems

Figure 4.1. Shadow of Mackenzie Place.
Source: Photo by Jesse Colin Jackson 2013.

unnecessary and perhaps illogical. The building was constructed when the population was half of what it is today. If it didn't meet an immediate need, then what was the aim in building it? "[N]ation-states often build infrastructures not to meet felt needs, but because those infrastructures signify that the nation-state is advanced and modern" (Anand, Gupta, and Appel 2018, 19; see also Ferguson 1999; Harvey and Knox 2015). In part, the High Rise helped to create an image of northern Canada as available for investment and development by being able to effectively house labour (workers). At the same time, the building put into practice emerging local and state policies that made land available for private sale and marked some Northern regions as white, or at least not exclusively Indigenous.

To understand why and how a tall, modern tower came to be built in a small subarctic town, it is important to understand some broad outlines of the history and geography of the area. The High Rise overlooks the town's namesake, the Hay River. The Hay River travels north from Alberta and connects to Great Slave Lake, one of the world's largest freshwater lakes. The mouth of the river provides for excellent fishing. As such, it was used seasonally by Dene peoples for thousands of years. Dene people fish and hunt and thus chose different sites in the region to make their livelihoods. Existing seasonal sites became more permanent dwellings for some Dene when the presence of the fur trade posts and missionaries began to take root. At Hay River, this started in the 1860s. Another distinguishing feature of the local landscape is a branch of the Hay River known as the West Channel. It departs from the Hay River and creates an island just off the lake's shore. This area is known today as Vale Island, or Old Town. At the turn of the twentieth century, settlements along the lake front on both sides of the river began to take shape (see map 3.1).

As Northern mining increased in the twentieth century, the Hay River area became increasingly important as a transportation hub. Three regional gold mines saw record profits when the end of Bretton Woods translated into fast-climbing gold prices.[1] Besides the gold boom, more "wealth" was imagined to be on its way. A proposed oil pipeline travelling through the territory would bring Arctic oil from the Beaufort Sea to southern markets. During these years, Hay River was completely redeveloped in preparation for what was imagined to be en route. Northern mining and mineral development found new vigour in 1958, with the election of a Conservative government. The new prime minister, John Diefenbaker, had a "Northern Vision" – prioritizing transportation and communication access to the region for industrial development – which led to his government's "Roads to Resources" policies (Isard 2010). The Canadian federal government funded infrastructure development, which led to the creation of these critical transportation nodes and networks that would make the Arctic's natural resources available to southern markets and bolster the country's economy and status as a "nature exporting society" (Coronil 1997, 7). The plan was abandoned by the 1960s, when Diefenbaker failed to be re-elected during a financial crisis. His Liberal successor reined in Northern infrastructure expenses. Nevertheless, some of the Northern Vision initiatives made their mark on the region, notably the 1964 development of the Mackenzie Northern Railway line, which

---

1 The Bretton Woods agreement and system created a collective international currency exchange regime based on the US dollar and gold. The agreement was between the United States, Canada, Australia, Japan, and several western European countries. In 1971, the US untethered the US dollar to gold. This began the dismantling of the agreement.

was intended to serve the new lead and zinc mining town of Pine Point, only seventy kilometres east of Hay River.

Even with the cancelled Roads to Resources initiatives, modern planning became the priority for Hay River after a 1963 flood damaged many of the homes and much of the infrastructure on Vale Island. During that time, new kinds of state planners (for example, human geographers) were sent to study the region and to help plan for a new town site (Zarchikoff 1975). For the state, Vale Island (the west bank) and the rest of the lakeshore were desirable due to their industrial development potential. The island was imagined as a shipyard for increased mineral exploration and development, not as a residential area. The plan was to move everyone away from the water's edge to a new town.

By the 1960s, the east bank had become predominantly Dene; the west bank was Métis and white. This racial divide of non-Indigenous on the west bank and Indigenous on the east side of the river was a recent development. The 1963 flood had also damaged the settlements on the east bank (then called Indian Village). A small social housing development for Treaty Indians (locally called Disneyland) was meant to encourage all people to move to the west side.[2] For the Dene, the "treaty houses" proved to be unpopular, as they were small and not on the waterfront. Another major issue was that very few couples consisted of two "Treaty" Indians (meaning having the same requisite legal status); therefore, they did not qualify for subsidized housing. Older members of the community, both Indigenous and not, will tell you that the planning and building of this new town was instrumental in shaping race relations today as it created more of a divide between the population than there had been before.

The High Rise was in the planned centre of Hay River's New Town on the west bank. It is an example of what anthropologist Brian Larkin (2013) calls "contemporaneous modernity," where infrastructure from elsewhere is brought into a rural place like Hay River in order to signal urbanization and produce a common visual conceptual paradigm

---

2 I tried many times to get a sense of where the term "Disneyland" came from and never was able to get an answer. The houses are small, cartoon-like almost. They are white, but each has (or had) a brightly coloured trim paint. One Elder who had lived there told me "everyone who lives there is dizzy!" and exploded laughing.

of what it means to be modern. A Toronto-based developer bought the key downtown lots and based the High Rise plans on British-imported designs increasingly common in Toronto in the 1960s. With the new pipeline project rumoured to be in the works, the building was imagined to accommodate the eventual influx of (white) labour. It was meant to showcase the North as a place with potential to be modern, a place where non-Indigenous people could live with city comforts.

During the middle decades of the twentieth century, high-modernist urban planning swept many parts of the globe (J.C. Scott 1999) and found its way to different Arctic and subarctic locales; Hay River was but one example. Matthew Farish and Whitney Lackenbauer (2009) have traced the connections between modernization theory and Cold War militarism in the communities of Inuvik (NWT) and Frobisher Bay (later renamed Iqaluit, Nunavut). Federal officials during these years "proposed ambitious urban models designed to simultaneously overcome the hostility of the northern environment and catapult native northerners into conditions of modern living" (Farish and Lackenbauer 2009, 517). Unlike other modernization schemes across the Arctic and subarctic, which were aimed at the Indigenous population, the High Rise was aimed at attracting a working middle class that was not yet necessarily in town. The so-called modern features of the town's development (recreation centre, multiple grocery stores) were, and are to this day, essential to drawing labour north. In this way, Hay River's infrastructure worked as a promise to capital that the North would be available for development while at the same time promising to settler Canadians from the south that they could lead a good life north of the sixtieth parallel.

DIVERGENCES

[Infrastructures] are formed with the moralities and materials of the time and political moment in which they are situated.

– Anand, Gupta, and Appel (2018, 6)

While the development of New Town and the High Rise more specifically were meant to beckon industry and a new middle class northwards, the results were largely mixed. Like with infrastructure of all kinds, different visions of the future and aspirations for one's own life play a role in how or if a project finds support among populations (Anand, Gupta, and Appel 2018, 19).

As you will see here, modernization efforts in Hay River involved the displacement and resettlement of the population. The High Rise, and its controversial reception by local people, must be understood within this broader context of displacement and dislocation. Both the idea of a "new town" and the High Rise found disapproval among Indigenous peoples, as well as many working-class whites who were largely working in the fishing industry.

For non-Indigenous working-class families living on Vale Island, new lots of land were offered as straight exchanges. However, the cost of servicing these new lots and taxes made them unaffordable to many residents. Those who had the means to relocate did so. Essentially, New Town divided the settler population by class position. New Town was nicknamed "Snob Hill" during those first decades, but little of this class antagonism is known today. These tensions over the large-scale changes in the community were palpable in all of the reporting from that era. In 1970, an aspiring photojournalist came to town and described Hay River this way:

> Tugboats and barges, freight trains and bush planes, trucks and bulldozers. That's Hay River, Northwest Territories. Man's country. Transportation hub of the north. Doorway to the western Arctic. End of steel for the CN's Great Slave Railway. Beginning of the Mackenzie River's trans-shipment lifeline. Hustle and Bustle. "It's also a town racked with the gaw-damdest growing pains," says mayor Don Stewart. "We've grown up so fast from a little Indian village to an up and coming boom town we don't know which direction we are heading."
> (Tasky 1971)

The development of New Town was not a happy story of progress, nor were these "natural" growing pains. These were class-based conflicts, shot through with racial tensions, that were indicative of the differentiated capacity for everyday people to make a living. Regional newspapers from the time report many complaints over the costs and unfair assignment of key pieces of property to non-local developers. Existing small-business owners on Vale Island could scarcely afford lots in New Town. While many tried to stay open in Old Town, as in-migrants came north in the 1970s and 1980s, more of the business activity moved to New Town. Today, there are only a handful of industrial businesses in Old Town. Residential lots do remain, and many people fondly call Old Town home. However, this part of town is not serviced in the same way (for example, there is no underground plumbing) and there are annual threats of flooding. The spatial divide of Old Town/New Town remains to this day highly classed; working-class people live primarily in Old Town while professional classes live in the newest subdivisions of New Town. Since Vale Island was partially zoned for industrial development, the rail yard and shipping headquarters for Northern Transportation Company Limited are located there, along with a few other shipping and construction-related businesses. The wealthiest people in town today are primarily settlers who acquired (or were given) larger, commercial lots in New Town upon original sale.

The 1963 flood energized the spatial and racial reorganization of the town; however, the motivations for architectural and infrastructural choices came from the expectations of a proposed pipeline being approved. While the pipeline was still being debated, investors began anticipating the needs of the forthcoming mega-project. While few local people had access to the substantial capital needed to engage with gas and mineral development directly, a small handful could participate in construction projects that facilitated industrial growth, like building or renewing roads and houses. In the 1960s and 1970s, much like today, the potential wealth of natural resources for locals was in building and maintaining infrastructures of extraction. Paving roads, building homes, draining lakes, and caring for workers and their families are key livelihood strategies for many Northerners. As has been the case since the arrival of missionaries, most of the wage work in Hay River was in construction and infrastructure development. While direct resource work often gets much of the academic attention, the important role local labour plays in constructing the future visions of state and capital cannot be underestimated. The most consistent work available to this day remains in construction and transportation. This work is sporadic, dangerous, and largely unregulated.

The High Rise was at its inception an instance of what I call "infrastructural prospecting" – meaning that in anticipation of the arrival of mega-projects, local and non-local investors stake claims on the kinds of supporting infrastructure those mega-projects may need. The importance of infrastructural prospecting struck me as I interviewed Albert, the first manager of the High Rise. In the 1970s, he left his position as the town's school bus driver to take the new job. He recalled the early years of the High Rise in a tone that tacked back and forth between enthusiasm and remorse. Now in his seventies, with weathered tattoos and living in a small modular home, Albert told me about the eagerness of local business owners to see the High Rise happen. Leaning in across the kitchen table, as if to share a secret, he said, "It was all about the town's 'big wheels,' you know what I mean? The Big Wheels wanted it. And they got it."

The term "big wheels" is a stand-in for non-Indigenous elites, who, in the 1960s and 1970s, were a small but financially powerful group of people. The exclusion of Indigenous people and working-class whites like Albert from this kind of infrastructural prospecting laid the groundwork for contemporary forms of socio-economic monitoring and impact-benefit agreements, which are aimed at widening just who could benefit from extractive development.

As Albert's comments about the big wheels reveal, the High Rise stood for a future very few local people wanted. The local newspaper referred to it as a "human filing cabinet." While the building owners advertised it as offering "modern, cosmopolitan living on par with cities like Calgary," local people saw it as an imposition that represented all that is wrong with urban life. For its supporters in the 1970s, the High Rise was a clear sign that the North was "ready" for development and modernization. However, during construction of the High Rise, plans for the pipeline were shelved as a result of Indigenous activism, a growing Canadian environmental movement, and the falling price of oil.

Holding a coffee mug that said "Believe" in cursive lettering, Albert described the High Rise as "a white elephant." In North America, "white elephant" is often a term used to refer to an expensive burden that fails to meet expectations.[3] The construction of the High Rise was

---

3 The expression, unknown to me at the time, was popularized following American circus man P.T. Barnum's experience with an elephant: he acquired the elephant after much effort and great expense, only to discover that his supposedly white elephant was actually dirty grey in colour with a few pink spots.

a feat in its own right. The company that built Toronto's CN Tower was brought in to erect the structure. Building materials had to be shipped in by rail, a process that was stalled when rail workers went on strike before all of the materials had arrived. The cost to build the High Rise was far more than anticipated. Occupancy once it was complete was much lower than expected, creating almost immediate financial problems. Albert described having to take materials like toilets from empty apartments on the lower floors to replace broken items in the occupied units. "There was no money left for upkeep, so I had to make do with what was around."

The High Rise was meant to house new middle-class professionals, which has not been its fate. As I will describe in detail in chapter 5, the building today is a near-perfect illustration of what sociologist John Porter (1965) calls the Canadian multicultural "vertical mosaic." Whereas Canadian multicultural rhetoric maintains that newcomers can preserve their cultural differences, Porter points out that these differences nevertheless are part of a racial hierarchy of privilege. In the High Rise, top units are renovated and have better views. These units are generally occupied by white public servants. Indigenous and immigrant renters tend to be clustered in poorly maintained units near the bottom. I was told explicitly by many people in town that I should try and get a unit on a higher floor to avoid "the worst of it."

Even if the building was and remains a financial disappointment (it has been sold five times since construction and has gone into receivership[4] more than once), it is part of the architecture of extraction in that it houses a "just in time" labour supply for resource booms and busts. It also manages to serve as an illustration of the "problems" that resource development is often said to solve. The High Rise illustrates how the architecture of extraction involves changes that seem distant from, or even unrelated to, mining. Local stakeholders hoping to profit from imagined development create structures (in this case, a physical building) that will long outlive the particular project that it is said to serve. At the same time, the building's meanings change over time and the sentiments that it engenders become entangled with how extraction is experienced in the present.

---

4 When a property has loans that they can't pay, a court may assign a "receiver" to operate all aspects of the property until the foreclosure lawsuit is settled.

DISAPPOINTMENTS

Although the Mackenzie Place High Rise sits on a relatively flat stretch of subarctic landscape and can be seen from seventy kilometres away, for many residents (both in the town and in the tower), it is often described as a sight better left unseen. Wearing out in ways common to postwar towers, the slow decay of building materials and of its internal functions have been expedited by four months of sub-zero winter temperatures, incessant sun in the summer months, and unpredictable rental income that ebbs and flows with the region's mineral and gas economy. The exterior paint is dull and chipping. Some balconies are now condemned. Signs warning tenants not to go out on the unstable concrete have been taped to sliding glass doors. Despite being in northern Canada, the units run incredibly hot in the winter. While there are thermostats in each unit, they are generally unresponsive to adjustment. Instead, radiator heat pumps a steady stream of warm air into units. I often had to crack open my balcony door just to help move the heavy air out. This heating system, while inefficient, would be incredibly costly to replace.

This is a pivotal moment in the history of the postwar tower in general and certainly of this one in particular. Such buildings are old enough to require substantial repair but not old enough to be seen as "historical." For many local people and visitors to the region, a weathered tower on a subarctic landscape fails to meet expectations about either industrial progress or natural purity of the sub/Arctic. The 2008 Lonely Planet travel guide for Canada called Hay River "hard-bitten," which caused quite a stir locally and was primarily blamed on the unsightly High Rise (Spitzer 2008).

For the Northern middle class, the material failures of the building are often blamed on tenants who are presumed to be transient and thus disinterested in the arts of domestic care. My two years in the High Rise proved otherwise. Most tenants took great care to have their apartments reflect them. Walls were adorned with neat rows photographs of friends and family. Surfaces might have a single knickknack made by a relative or Northern craftsperson: a birch bark basket, a stone carving of a bear. The upkeep of the units was an opportunity for self-expression but was equally a way for some tenants to distance themselves from the accusations that all High Rise residents were, as one of my interlocutors put it, "riff-raff." Many tenants I interviewed described the building as "ghetto" and maintained that they would not be living there for long. An important part of being in the High Rise was expressing that you didn't truly belong there.

Tenants expressed many disappointments with the accommodations in the High Rise. Most glaringly was having to pay a rental price near double the national average for a unit in disrepair. Other disappointments seemed small but gained weight by their everydayness, like trying to get through the narrow entranceway with large bags of groceries and tripping on peeling linoleum tiles.

> or having to evacuate when the aging fire alarm goes off, again,
> or having to wait for 10 minutes for an elevator because the other one
> is out of service, again,
> or having to hear couples fights and trying to decide "how serious"
> it is and whether you should react,
> again.

As anthropologist Christina Schwenkel (2015) writes, "infrastructure, broken or not, often evokes a multiplicity of embodied sensations across the human sensorium." While tenants expressed many laments about the physical state of the building and the behaviour of their fellow residents, there were intimacies afforded by the thin walls and slow, cramped elevator everyone had to use. I remember one afternoon when my collaborator and I entered one of the two elevators and a tenant, a man in his fifties, said, "I guess this isn't the one?" His eyes ran over the perimeter of the scratched shellacked wood-panelled elevator walls. He continued, "Guy said an elevator was covered in blood this morning. Blood everywhere." The man was in the building while on a short work contract to install stucco ceiling at the new hospital. For newcomers, these visceral events, and possible traces left in the elevator, offered an opportunity to engage. "I hear it wasn't no one from the building," he added. We then noticed three thin dark red streaks on the door close to the bottom.

For the rest of that day, everyone will use elevator exchanges to try to piece together what could have happened. Those who sit and smoke at the picnic table out front will get pieces of the story from the property managers, who are out watering their struggling plants. One manager repeats the same joke to each passerby, "Twenty-three hours of sunshine. You think this shit would grow faster." His wife hauls a green watering can in and out of their ground-floor unit. These events and others that were much more serious (domestic violence ending in death, people falling from balconies, physical fights in the parking lot) drew people's curiosity and criticism. Who or what was responsible for these types of violence?

These spectacular events (although less common than people reported) as well as the kinds of everyday difficulties I described above are what people wanted to discuss most with me. It became clear through countless interviews that these concerns were not interpreted as failures of expedited resource development but of the building itself. People, for the most part, wanted out. But there was nowhere to go. It is in the wanting to leave the High Rise that high-wage work in mining comes to make sense. For the underemployed, to secure work in a mine was often a stated goal. For the professional-class tenants, their time in the building and in the community was to amass "experience" that could be used to bolster their chances of finding a job elsewhere and moving on. In this way, disappointment with infrastructure is an essential part of the Arctic's architecture of extraction, but more in a way that testifies to the volatility and exploitation of extractivism than to its straightforward progress.

Disappointment in Hay River's "modernization" plan as soon as it was complete indicated a kind of desire for different development. People become more invested in participating in (and not negating) extraction as they work to shape a future that aligns with their self-image. Disappointment creates a sense of wanting an otherwise, a collective feeling of "not this kind of future but another one." Over the thirty years since the New Town development, middle-class aesthetics in the North and in most Canadian cities moved away from modern towers and towards suburban homes. This is replicated in the NWT, with modular builds brought into town on the backs of flatbed trucks and snapped into place like Lego toys. The High Rise was part of a program to introduce private property as a concept and it in turn set in place the conditions for new forms of aspiring that are precisely what animate contemporary relationships to the diamond industry.

CONCLUSION

More often than not, when I told anyone that I was in town for re-search and living in the High Rise I would be told, "that's not the *real* Hay River!" As I mentioned in the introduction, Hay River is some-times described as "not the real North" on account of its physical location (one of the southernmost communities in the NWT) and its population being half non-Indigenous. How can spaces like a trans-portation community so crucial to national and global economic mar-kets be considered "not the real" North? How can a good segment of the working class be considered "not the real" Hay River? How can a building that can be seen from anywhere in the community be interpreted as separate from it? The aim of this chapter has not been to convince you of the "realness" of this structure or of its inhabit-ants. Rather, I wanted to show how infrastructure like the High Rise is a key component in the architecture of extraction. It is essential to natural resource development not only for the physical affordances it brings (allowing more people to move north) but also for the ways in which it is tangled up with legal and affective realms of life in the region by shaping debates over what the future should look like.

The High Rise isn't the only contested symbol in Hay River. In June 2009, Canada Post released a stamp of the Hay River inuksuk statue as part of their "Roadside Attractions" series featuring "quirky" ob-jects from each of Canada's ten provinces and three territories. On a Monday lunch hour that summer, seven local politicians, two postal workers, a lone stamp collector, and an anthropologist gathered in the town hall for the launch of a new stamp. The collection, according to a Canada Post representative in Ottawa, was meant to "speak to the fun of the countryside." More than that, the regional postal manager remarked,

> Canada Post's stamps attempt to capture Canada and what it means to be Canadian and showcase it to the world. [The Hay River stamp] celebrates a remarkable landmark that is fundamentally Canadian and speaks to who we are as a people." (CBC 2009)

Although the local stamp collector was happy to see his town rec-ognized on a stamp for the first time, he was not certain that the statue represented "the real" Hay River. He told the local paper, "Inukshuks are an ancient Inuit tradition of building stone markers to guide travellers through the landscape of the Far North." Hay River is not the "traditional" home of Inuit and by extension not the "natural" home of inuksuit. His comment was about possible cultural appropriation and "misrepresentation" of the community.

The town erected the inuksuk within the same decade as the High Rise construction. In 1978, Hay River co-hosted the first Arctic Winter Games, a sporting competition among regions from around the circumpolar world. The inuksuk was part of the process to mark the community as "Northern" in preparation for the event.[5] Like the High Rise, the meaning of the inuksuk is debated. The struggle over meaning is what is anthropologically interesting. When there are different ideas of what words or objects mean, the intricacies of power are revealed (Voloshinov 1973). My own observations suggest that while the High Rise and the inuksuk attempt to suggest distinct divides between past and future, tradition and modern, nature and development, Indigenous and migrant, the space between these dyads erodes in the daily life of the town and the debates about its future. Their instability as northern symbols makes clear that debates over Canada's North are not limited to land, property, and subsurface rights. Instead, competing visions for the region are worked out in relationship to infrastructure that emerged in relation to extractive impulses of the past but somehow stand apart from them in the present.

Literary theorist Terry Eagleton (2003, 87) writes, "Critics discuss symbols, while theorists ask by what mysterious process one thing comes to stand for another." Here I am raising a question about the impossibility of one thing (the High Rise) standing for another (the Arctic). While inuksuit have come to symbolize the Arctic, and sometimes Canada more broadly, urbanizing centres and structures north of the sixtieth parallel are semiotically immiscible with notions of "the North." The development of the High Rise, the town of Hay River, and its infrastructure are all key components in making Arctic resources

---

5 Hay River co-hosted the games with the nearby community of Pine Point, a town built around a lead-zinc mine. For the purpose of the games, the newly built rail line between the two communities – usually reserved for extraction-related cargo – was used to move athletes and other passengers between sites. Not since has there been rail passenger service anywhere in the region.

accessible to global markets. Part of the changes were physical, like building a railroad, paving a highway, and providing housing for incoming labour. Other changes have been less easy to see but are no less significant. This includes changes in dispositions and sentiments towards resource extraction. These come to matter a great deal. Affective and physical infrastructures are impossible to untangle.

DISCUSSION QUESTIONS

1 Describe an object that is symbolic of someone or something significant to you but bears no resemblance to that person, thing, or experience.
2 The chapter describes the High Rise and the inuksuk as somewhat failed symbols. Can you think of an example from your experience where something that was meant to symbolize something else failed to do so?
3 The chapter describes how expectations for the North that came from outside of it ended up shaping the town's infrastructure. Have others' expectations played a role in your life experiences? How so? Is that necessarily negative or positive?
4 Many tenants in the High Rise express that they don't like living there and will be leaving soon. Sometimes our identities are shaped and maintained by the things we distance ourselves from just as much as they are about the things we align with. Are there examples you can think of where you, or someone you know, explicitly distanced themselves from certain people, practices, or places in order to express their sense of identity and belonging?

CHAPTER FIVE

Mobility

The process of "preparing the Arctic" for diamond mining began well before prospectors confirmed the presence of gemstones beneath the tundra. In the nineteenth century, race and citizenship became, and remain, essential elements of the architecture of extraction. They arrange rights to property in a way that makes resources accessible to transnational capital, even if that access is often contentious. The configurations of race, space, and citizenship outlined in the previous chapters allowed for the creation of semi-urban "hubs" like Hay River that connect north and south through new transportation infrastructure like railroads, highways, and river barges. These hubs also enabled substantial in-migration. The twentieth century was marked by a steady increase of people moving to Northern hubs from nearby Indigenous villages, from across Canada, and from around the world (see figure 5.1). The ability to attract and absorb labour from other parts of the country and the world is a critical element of the architecture of the extractive industry. At the same time, natural resource activity waxes and wanes. Therefore, having a mobile labour force that moves on at a project's end is also critical. Just as emplacement (fixing people to a place) is critical to the architecture of extraction, so too is mobility.

Mining projects in sparsely populated regions are often associated with a transient workforce. What I learned from my years in northern Canada is that the different types of mobilities on which Arctic extraction depends are not captured by the stereotype of men brought in

Figure 5.1. View from Mackenzie Place window facing west.
Source: Photo by Jesse Colin Jackson 2013.

to work in the mines. Mobilities in northern Canada are diverse with respect to gender, class, ethnicity, economic sector, and time spent in the region.

What are the different types of mobilities involved in Arctic extractive industries in Canada? How is mobility part of the architecture of extraction? In order to illustrate the complex structures of mobility on which extraction depends, I share the trajectories of a diverse set of High Rise tenants to the Northern transportation hub of Hay River. Some are from as far away as the Philippines, while others are from Canada's Atlantic provinces. Some people, like Destiny, had only moved from the other side of the river. Their experiences reveal the types of conjunctures that bring together a labour supply "just in time" for resource booms and busts. I moved into the High Rise partly out of ethnographic curiosity. I wanted to get a clear picture of the kinds of people coming north to try their luck in a booming economy. Though I had lived in Hay River prior to taking on this research, I had no clear sense of who might live in the High Rise. This chapter centres on the stories of some of the people I met while living in the building. Taken together, their trajectories reveal that different scales and types of mobility are essential components in the architecture of extraction and reveal how the necessary architectures of extraction – like race, citizenship, and mobility – are at once physical, legal, structural, and aspirational.

GLOBAL SOUTH TO GLOBAL NORTH

What role does international immigration play in the Arctic's architecture of extraction? Over the course of my fieldwork, I learned that during resource highs, lower-wage work in the service sector becomes harder to fill as local people do their best to move into higher-wage work while they can. In the capital city of Yellowknife, I attended several events for local business owners to learn about federal programs to bring in international migrants for work in restaurants, shops, and hotels. These programs are not designed for resource extraction but are certainly integral to it. The 2016 census reported 3,690 immigrants total in the Northwest Territories. Most of these arrived during the diamond boom. While this may seem like a small number, it is a substantial portion of a relatively small overall population of around 44,000 people. This is particularly true in the capital city and hubs like Hay River and Inuvik, where the bulk of the immigrant population lives. What I learned in talking to Ivan Zuniga, an immigrant to the NWT, was that the practice of immigrants in service sector work was not an altogether new phenomenon. While it is often assumed that in-migration is linked to contemporary diamond activity, Ivan is part of a larger cohort of about 700 immigrants who arrived in the NWT before the 1980s (Government of Canada 2016).

Ivan moved to Hay River from Chile in 1978. His apartment had the identical layout as mine, yet it felt unfamiliar. The walls were filled with neatly framed family photographs and posters of airplanes. Ivan's eleven-year-old son stood hiding behind the front door as I arrived and quickly took off to a friend's apartment. Ivan sat down, crossed his legs, and began to tell me about his thirty years in the Northwest Territories.

Ivan's sister, Maria, was the first one to come to Canada from Chile. She had been working in Chile as a waitress in a Canadian-owned copper mine when she met her future husband, Dave, a driller from

Manitoba. When Chilean president Allende came to power in 1970, he nationalized the copper industry and Dave was transferred to a mine in Flin Flon, Manitoba. Unsatisfied with the work, Maria and her husband moved west, eventually ending up in Hay River, where Dave became a fisherman and entrepreneur. Ivan and his parents came to Canada to console Maria after Dave died by suicide. It was 1978 and Chilean military dictator Pinochet had come to power, so fleeing Chile appealed to the family for various reasons.

Ivan explained his first impressions to me this way: "Being an immigrant and coming up here is like winning the [lottery]. When we arrived, they were desperate for help. Dad took a job as a janitor for $1,000 a week and could not believe it! Although my father had been wealthy in Chile and had owned his own business, he did not mind being the janitor because he was still treated like a 'mister.' We became servants, but we were well-treated, so that was confusing to us."

In 1979, the nearby Pine Point lead and zinc mine just east of Hay River was in full swing. Ivan got a job as a mill operator for $12.20 an hour. While employed, the company paid for his room and board. He stayed for three and a half years. He told me about the strength of his union at that time: the United Steelworkers. They taught him about coffee breaks and got him an English tutor. These are two lessons he said he was still grateful for. "I was mostly working with Native guys," said Ivan, "some from Manitoba, some from Fort Resolution. That's how I know so many Elders from there. Those guys were all at Pine Point working the day shifts at the sawmill."

Ivan's observations about his co-workers are important. Contemporary forms of Indigenous participation in resource industries are not by any means new, even as prospective resource projects and ethics campaigns attempt to configure mining as a new possibility for Indigenous gain. Their participation in mining should not be taken as a sign that they had stopped engaging in subsistence activities like hunting and fishing. Just the opposite. As Sahlins (1999) and, more recently, Dombrowski (2008, 2010) have shown, those who are most successful at subsistence activities are usually equally successful at procuring waged employment. After the 1870s, people needed cash to access the means of production. Unlike the pre-1950s, when goods could be acquired through debt from fur posts, the more recent need for access to tools (guns, shells, fuel) requires access to wages, whether directly or indirectly.

During a recession, the mine took a six-week closure. Ivan had wanted to move up to surface work and took the closure as an opportunity to move on. When the mine reopened, he was re-offered his position, but he turned it down in favour of pursuing his diploma for motor vehicle licensing and instruction. Ivan rattled off a long list of the career changes that took him all over the Territories. He had tried owning a restaurant in Yellowknife with his wife but ended up back in Hay River when it did not get off the ground. "We were happy to come back to Hay River. It's friendly here. At first, I thought it was creepy, weird, but now I think it's special."

At the time of the interview, Ivan was a truck driver for one of the largest ground shipping companies in the region. He had been with the company long enough to primarily go on short-haul day trips. His load was usually groceries and mail destined for different communities on the same side of the lake as Hay River. Ivan's marriage was in trouble and that was what landed him in the High Rise. He had faith that God would bring him and his wife back together again.

Since Ivan's arrival in the late 1970s, the number of immigrants to the Northwest Territories has tripled, making Northern locals more multicultural than ever before and undoing the simple binary of Indigenous and non-Indigenous Northerners. At the decade around the discovery and boom in Northern diamonds, over 500 people immigrated to the Northwest Territories from the Philippines alone. Mirroring Canada's general immigration trends, the Philippines is a prominent source of international labour.

Chris had been in Canada for seven years and had not once returned home.[1] He emailed me to set up his interview and I could not place his name from his message, although I had been in the building for six months by the time I put up recruitment flyers. I had never seen him before the day I showed up at his two-bedroom apartment on the third floor. In a spare bedroom he had set up a recording studio where he sang and recorded Filipino folk songs, as well as original works in what he simply referred to as "my language." He would send the CDs he recorded to his wife and children, who still lived in the Philippines.

---

1 This is his choice of term for the Philippines.

From our conversation, I learned that Chris had trained as an engineer and worked in the capital city of Manila before graduating. He then went to Saudi Arabia for five years to work for a German company. He used his savings to return home in the late 1980s and started a small business, which then failed. He arrived in Canada to work for Magna, an automotive systems company. He thought he was going to work in Toronto but was told by his employer that he was "mis-oriented" and would need "Canadian experience" for those positions. It is a common occurrence that immigrants to Canada with advanced degrees struggle to gain employment suited to their abilities. Employers often state the lack of "Canadian experience" to justify hiring immigrants at a lower-level salary than they might otherwise deserve (Allan 2014).

Chris was given a job in Magna's factory in St. Thomas, Ontario; he held it for two years before being laid off. He took a job at a local fast-food chain. He described it as being "a little bit embarrassing" when he told me that he kept the job in order to support his family. When he saw a six-month contract with the NWT power corporation, he applied for it. He was on his second six-month contract. Full-time employment with the power company was among the most coveted jobs in town. Although Chris could qualify as a "Northerner" on paper, in practice this was unlikely to yield permanent work for him. This has to do, in part, with local politics, but also the way Chris' "marked" English was perceived by his employer to be a barrier to full employment. Although he was extremely proficient in English, Chris seemed certain that without learning to minimize his "accent," he would never get a better position. He often asked me for English lessons, as ESL courses were unavailable in town.

Although there is a rather large Filipino community in both Hay River and Yellowknife, there are often moments when they are reminded that they are "not really a Northerner" or maybe not even "really Canadian." For instance, at the French-language school where I worked, many children have Filipino mothers and Francophone fathers.[2] The French school is a politically contentious issue I have

---

2 Many of these women came to Canada as care workers in the late 1980s. A few began their careers in the neighbouring mine town of Pine Point. There, they met their husbands, as Francophone men are typically overrepresented in the primary industries (Heller and Bell 2012). Once the Pine Point mine closed, many families moved to Hay River. Some Filipino women work in the service industry (e.g., as grocery clerks) or run home daycare programs.

described in detail elsewhere (Heller and Bell 2012; see also Heller 1999). The short version is that federal law mandates that school instruction be offered in both official languages (French and English) if there is a demand. In the 1990s, Francophone parents organized, lobbied for, and won the right to a school. School funding is on a per-capita basis. Some Anglophone school officials and local people feel that this process "steals" money from their schools. This sense is further compounded by the belief that most of the students "aren't really" Francophone, as most of these students speak English at home. During my fieldwork, this issue had reached a boiling point. An Anglophone school board representative ordered that the court verify all Francophone students' so-called authenticity. The accusation was that the French school was "making" Francophones. The major evidence against the school that I heard in casual conversation was stated in the form of a question: "How can all those Filipino kids be French?!"[3] These tensions, and Chris's experiences with limited job mobility, reveal how immigrants have been central to Northern economic development for some time and yet face barriers to their integration and access to the "good life" Northern booms are said to offer those willing to travel long distances for work.

NATIONAL MOVEMENTS

International immigration to Northern locales is on the rise globally (Dybbroe, Dahl and Müller-Wille 2010; Orttung 2016); however, the majority of in-migration to the Northwest Territories is from other parts of Canada – particularly flows of people coming from the east to the (north)west. The 2000s were marked by a heavy flow of workers from Canada's eastern provinces to resource-rich regions like the NWT and Alberta. Historically, people from the island province of Newfoundland have been overrepresented in those on the move (On the Move Partnership, n.d.; Palmer and Sinclair 2000). The collapse of the fishing industries that long sustained the province created a large

---

3 For a dynamic discussion of contemporary issues with respect to Filipinos in Canada, see Coloma et al. (2012).

labour pool that the rest of Canada drew on for construction and extraction sectors in times of expedited growth. Newfoundlanders are culturally and linguistically distinct from other Canadians and are often seen as fun-loving and humorous. These stereotypes, although positive, often obscure the difficult paths those from Newfoundland must follow in order to access some economic stability. The story of Billy makes this clear.

Billy showed up to my apartment for his interview with six cans of Molson Canadian beer, a bottle of white wine, and a small bottle of Root Beer Schnapps. He was one of the seven men who immediately responded to the participant recruitment flyers I slipped under the High Rise's eighty-five apartment doors. I often saw Billy at the local pub when he was on his "out" rotation from one of the mines. He worked in logistics, which I understood to roughly translate to putting things and people in the right places around the worksite and camp. In the interview, his speech style wavered from wildly excited to quiet and conspiratorial. It was clear that he felt vulnerable about leaking any information about the mines that could get him into trouble. "They really keep tabs on you, you know," he said out of the corner of his mouth.

Billy was over fifty years old, and his trajectory maps neatly onto some of the major Canadian economic shifts that took place during his lifetime. He was an athlete in high school in Newfoundland, leaving early to start work in the marine shipping industry. With declining codfish stocks in the early 1980s, his parents moved to Toronto to work in manufacturing industries. Billy joined them after having put in ten hard years of work at sea. He took a job in the meatpacking industry in the early 1980s. When the industry began to "modernize" and larger companies merged with one another, meatpacking plants were relocated or "updated," so as to reduce the numbers of unionized employees. When he heard the news about diamonds in the NWT in the mid-1990s, he knew where to go to find better work.

When he arrived in Hay River, he spent his first years in the shipping industry. Northwest Transportation Company Limited (NTCL) had its headquarters in Hay River. NTCL started in the 1950s as a federal shipping company linked to the uranium mine project on Great Bear Lake. When demand for uranium dropped, the government of Canada split the company, and the shipping division became an entity in its own right. Now owned by the Inuvialuit Regional Corporation, NTCL provides marine transportation services to communities and resource exploration projects along the Mackenzie River in the Northwest Territories and across the western Arctic. The shipping season is typically five months long if rivers stay clear of ice. Deckhands and office employees tend to be hired locally, while other labour is brought in, primarily from Newfoundland. Billy worked the boats for his first summer, and then actively pursued a job with the mines as a more permanent employment option.

Billy got a job with a local automotive company that held multiple contracts with the mines (auto parts, service, vehicle operation, etc.). Part of his company's winning bid proposal is their claim to a 100 per cent Northern employee rate. Since Billy had an address and had been in the territories for three months, he was considered a "Northerner" and eligible to be hired. He spoke with slight frustration about the policy. On the one hand, it had given him a leg up to get into the mines, but now he felt like he was stuck in Hay River. He had wanted to move back to Newfoundland and fly back and forth like many of the other subcontractors, but giving up his address would mean giving up his job, as the 100 per cent Northern employee policy was strictly enforced, at least at his level.

Billy had been saving for quite some time, and he bought his first home (a small trailer) the winter after we initially spoke. I would pass him on the street occasionally, and at one point he let me know that his job position was more vulnerable than he had initially communicated. Additionally, owning a home made him more concerned about keeping a steady job. In late May 2009, he told me that the workforce at the mine had been cut in half. His job was considered part of the site's maintenance, so regardless of whether it was in production or not, he was still needed. Still, he was concerned because the mines were increasingly ending subcontracts. He had heard of some workers being let go by the subcontractor and then wooed back by the mine directly; these were not the circumstances he could count on. He was doing his best to do his "top performance" on each and every shift. Billy's trajectory makes clear that a large part of Canada's citizenry is "indispensably disposable" (Kawashima 2009).

In the 2000s, migration from other parts of the east coast of Canada began to rise (Heller et al. 2015). In particular, the bilingual province of New Brunswick became a key source of labour for Northern development. Gary arrived from the maritime province of New Brunswick in 2008. Gary's booming voice and assertive stance stood in stark contrast to the Seven Dwarfs sweatshirt he wore to my apartment on a Sunday afternoon in August. He sat in a wing chair with his feet thrown over the right arm. He was in town on a contract to install sprinklers in a newly built assisted-living facility.

Two years earlier, Gary was living in his car in Woodstock, New Brunswick, when a contractor picked him up to work as labour on a job at the local hospital. A few days into the job, the boss realized that Gary would have to be registered as an apprentice. The hospital was a government project, and in New Brunswick all provincial projects require labourers be enrolled as apprentices to accumulate hours towards professional certification. When the job ended, Gary had worked enough hours to write his first block of apprentice tests. He was delighted when he passed, but his excitement quickly dissipated, as the employer would not take him back due to the legislated wage increase that comes with training.[4]

While on the job site, Gary worked with someone who did contract work in the Northwest Territories. Gary's new contact had passed along information for a company that did similar work to Gary's new trade: sprinkler installation. With his unemployment payments dwindling, Gary sent a resume to Yellowknife. That same day he got a call from the employer with an offer to fly him up the following day. He explained it this way:

> Well, I am single, right, and I don't care and I'm tired of not paying my payments. I'm tired of Honda Canada calling me everything but a delinquent, right. I'm tired of having surcharges at the Royal Bank. I said yes. I had no idea. I'm not world travelled. I am 51 years old, and I had never been on an airplane in my life. Well, that next day I took three!

His first project was putting in a sprinkler system at a power plant in a diamond mine. Largely, he enjoyed the work. "It's awesome," he said. "The food is next to none." He did note that there were a few

---

4 This was Gary's interpretation of what happened. He explained that there had been four of them in the same situation and none were given their positions back.

downsides. Speaking about security and safety procedures he noted, "In a way, it's a glorified jail. The only difference is if you screw up, you get kicked out. But I had a good experience." When his first three weeks were complete, he was flown home, where he collected unemployment insurance until he got another call from Yellowknife. Now on a second contract in Hay River, Gary enjoyed the high salary he was earning. He put it this way:

> Well, that is what I am here for. The money, not anything else…. I get awesome pay: $18 an hour. Plus, for every hour I work safely, I get one dollar put in a kitty for me. I can cash it in anytime I want to buy tools. I get a food allowance of $55 a day. I work two hours of overtime every day and I work every Saturday … it works for me because I have nobody to care for but myself and I can go anywhere on a minute's notice.[5]

Gary's employer was paying for his High Rise apartment. His wage (without overtime) was actually on the lower end for the North, but compared to New Brunswick, it was extremely high. Because Gary did not have to pay to subsist in the North, he found his temporary stay quite comfortable, yet his participation in the Northern economy puts downward pressure on wages. At the job's end, he had accumulated 1,200 hours of work; he was able to go back on unemployment and prepare to write the second block of apprenticing exams. Northern diamond development today, much like gold mining in the 1930s, depends on the uneven development of capitalism globally. Economic decline in other parts of the country becomes gains for Northern employers, as workers like Gary are made available at lower wages than local people. While the Northern economy depends on this unevenness, it can't fully control it or produce as needed.

Not all national migrants come to work directly in resource sectors. Many people move north to fill public sector jobs (teaching, health care) that reproduce the expanded population. This work isn't secondary to mining, it is essential to it. Most of this work is done by women, and yet I learned that most women in the High Rise did not

---

5 Here and elsewhere, I use ellipses (…) to indicate that I have edited out sections of the interview for clarity and brevity.

see themselves as integral to local economy, or as "labour migrants" at all. When I slid participant recruitment flyers under all eighty-five apartment doors at the High Rise asking to talk about experiences of "labour migration" I heard back from only men (with the exception of two of my female friends). Through subsequent conversations with women, I learned many High Rise women did not identify with the call, on the grounds that "labour" is understood as primary resource jobs or other types of masculinized work. Most women, save one left-leaning migrant from France, would not consider themselves or their work as "labour," although they all worked both in and outside of the home. Many of them had indeed moved for reasons related to work. Marion's story sheds light on this gendered aspect of national migration.

Marion pulled up to the High Rise in a Ford Focus station wagon in November. Her possessions filled the back half of the car. In the passenger seat was Sadie, her French bulldog, dressed in a sailor's costume. Marion was one of four new tenants in the High Rise who had come to work as nurses or nurses' aides in the new assisted living facility where Gary was installing sprinklers. Marion was close to retirement and felt financially underprepared. She was a registered practical nurse (RPN) working in Ontario and had come up north in the early 1990s to earn the higher salaries afforded to Northern and rural public servants. She had saved enough to return to Ontario and buy a house. However, over the course of her four years in the North, the conditions of work in health care provision had changed significantly. Casual contracts had become commonplace. In the 1960s, nursing in Canada was characterized by strong worker organization. As Guy Standing (2011) notes, the increased contractualization of labour means that collective contracts in industrial societies are increasingly replaced by individual ones. This allows for employers to provide different levels of security to their workers. Marion, upon her return to Ontario took a string of casual positions, hoping they were each only temporary. Coming from a relatively small town, there were few full-time openings for Marion, and when a full-time employee left, a contract worker would take their position. This strategy of using enormous amounts of contract or casual labour is what is referred to in business-speak as "functional flexibility." According to Standing (2011, 56), "the essence of functional flexibility is to make it possible for firms to change the division of labour quickly without cost and to shift workers between tasks and positions and workplaces."

The deterioration of conditions of work in other parts of the country is a large part of why people move north. This was certainly the case for many teachers and nurses I spoke with over the course of my time in the field. This was also the case in my own experience. When I finished my teaching degree, Ontario had little in the way of full-time employment and was in the process of imposing new types of scrutinizing measures upon teachers' work (standardized testing, professionalization credits, etc.). Marion and I both travelled from Ontario for similar reasons. The North's public sector depends on in-migrants to be fully staffed. To be able to recruit people to come from elsewhere, it must offer lucrative contracts and not casual ones. The deterioration of public sector employment is much less acute in the Territories than elsewhere and therefore the region is successful in drawing people northwards. These movements cause friction as these stable, well-paying jobs are coveted and, in many ways, exclude local (specifically Indigenous) people from holding them as they require education that isn't offered locally. There have been efforts to try and certify local nurses and teachers through programs that require less time in "the south" but this remains a vexed issue.

INDIGENOUS MIGRATION

In Canada, migration and Indigenous Studies are usually held as distinct concerns. Much of the research on Northern migration in particular treats Indigenous and non-Indigenous migration as separate issues. It has even been argued that these two disparate phenomena require different methodological approaches (Cooke and Bélanger 2006; Petrov 2007). Northern migration research generally has one of two emphases: either a focus on the migration of Indigenous bodies out of the North to urban centres in the south (Newhouse and Peters 2003) or on non-Indigenous labour in-migration (Heleniak 1999; Zarchikoff 1975). All deploy the same oppositional understanding (see Nugent 1994) of Indigenous and non-Indigenous and all posit migration as a problem. Urbanization of Indigenous populations is described in relation to its burden on social welfare and housing programs (Kuhn and Sweetman 2002) and non-Indigenous migration is described as an issue of an "unstable labour force" (Heleniak 1999). In most instances, the primary unit of analysis is the "ethnic group," often termed "community."

As noted by Glick Schiller (2012, 66), "The problematic framing of migration research in terms of ethnic groups within nation-states obscures the effects of the global restructuring of capital on the population, both migrant and non-migrant, in a specific locality." This became especially clear to me as I met many people who were both migrants to the NWT and Indigenous. Like their non-Indigenous counterparts from regions of Canada in economic decline, Indigenous people were arriving in the North to access the benefits of the diamond boom. Many of the men I spoke with were experienced equipment operators and had no trouble getting work in the mines. Corporate social responsibility campaigns make mines eager to have these skilled Indigenous bodies filling positions (even if they were non-local). Indigenous migrants, an important subset of the population involved in extraction, are made invisible by corporate and state impact assessment measures that assume clear dichotomies between Indigenous and not and between migrant and local. Trevor's experiences in moving north show what it means to be both Indigenous and migrant.

As described in the introduction, Trevor's family moved to the Northwest Territories when Trevor's father took a job helping to build one of the diamond mines. A year later, his parents divorced. His father moved on to a different job in another part of the country, while Trevor's mom decided to stay and raise her two boys in the North. While I was there, Trevor and his mom, Cindy, also lived in the High Rise. Cindy excitedly talked to me about the big opportunity Trevor had by being enrolled in the mining course I described in the introduction. As a reminder, Trevor is Métis, but non-local. That means he had the requisite citizenship status to enrol in a program designated as for Indigenous people even though he wasn't exactly who they had in mind when they designed the course. When Trevor introduced himself on the first day of the mining class, he described himself as being "at a crossroad." Pulling a red New York Yankees hat over his eyes, he said, "either I continue on the path I am on, getting in trouble, jail and shit, or I turn myself around with one of these jobs." The stakes for Trevor's success were high. I will continue his story in the next chapter, which focuses on the training course he was so optimistic about.

Other Indigenous mobilities were much shorter but no less significant. Michelle had moved to Hay River and the High Rise from a nearby Indigenous community. Michelle was thirty years old and two semesters from completing her high school diploma. "I am sick of planning for my future," she told me in our brief interview. She was one of eight young mothers who lived in the High Rise. I met her at the Hay River community college. Before teaching the work readiness course I describe in chapter 5, I was invited to talk to the college students – all women – about being a woman in university. It was supposed to be motivational. Tim, the college director, felt that many of the women were very close to moving on but that for some reason, they continued to drag their feet close to graduation or in the application stage for university. My job was to help them make a five-year plan. During my best effort to provide a non-condescending and informative talk, most of the women looked completely unimpressed. In a one-on-one conversation later, Michelle explained her feelings on the matter; "I mean, you spend all this time planning out what to do, and you think, okay, this is going to work. Then, of course, something happens, and you are right back where you started. It's a waste of time, all these plans."

Michelle had two children who were in primary school. After talking for some time, she let me know that she was expecting again, and that was why she was so resistant to committing to more courses. She explained, "my boyfriend is looking for full-time work now and that means in the mines. He will have to do two weeks in, two weeks out. I can't go to school and raise three kids when I will be alone half of the time." I asked her about other employment possibilities for her boyfriend, but she was adamant: "The mines pay really well; we will be able to get ahead." Michelle did not return to the college for her final semester of her GED. In the new year, she and her family left the High

Rise and moved in with her parents. Her boyfriend had not had much luck getting a job in the mines, so they needed to cut expenses before the baby arrived.

Extraction-driven Indigenous migration in Arctic countries continues to be an understudied phenomenon. The romantic idea that Indigenous people are fixed in place means that questions of mobility are sidelined to research that reinforces a focus on local attachments to place. This work is of value insofar as it is usually an important part of Indigenous claims to land and livelihood; however, these same processes of emplacement cannot be fully understood without looking at the concomitant forms of mobility that emerge at the same time.

CONCLUSION

I was not alone in my initial murky understanding of High Rise residents. Marie, one of the local school principals, had lived in Hay River for ten years, yet she had never been in the High Rise before I moved in. After visiting me a few times, she declared, "There are people here I have never seen before in my life. This place is a separate culture!" Yet "High Rise culture" has never made it onto an ethno-cultural map of the Northwest Territories. Unlike so-called local traditional cultures, it is not written up as a tourist attraction or described as a source of pride. No one, not even its tenants, would tell you that the High Rise is "the real" Hay River. With only a few exceptions, most tenants spend their time distancing themselves from High Rise culture rather than embracing it. Although High Risers may not self-identify as being part of a coherent cultural whole, they are extremely insightful with respect to questions of political economy. From the perspective of my eighth-floor apartment, and through my interactions with High Risers, crucial components of Canadian political economy – present and past – come into view. Specifically, their mobilities provide a vantage point from which to understand larger questions of social mobility and reproduction on which the architecture of Arctic extraction depends.

DISCUSSION QUESTIONS

1 Migration is sometimes discussed as resulting from push/pull factors. Were there examples of migration stories that centred on being pushed out of their home community/country? What about examples of pull factors? Are there any stories that don't neatly fit the push/pull model?

2 Consider Destiny's different mobilities described in chapter 2 as compared to the examples in chapter 5. In what ways are her experiences like any others described? How do they diverge?

3 The tenants of the High Rise don't see themselves as a coherent whole. Nevertheless, do they share anything in common with one another?

4 Indigenous migrants are often seen as anomalous in Canada even though their numbers are rising. What does their interpretation as anomalous tell us about broad settler Canadian expectations for/of Indigenous people?

CHAPTER SIX

Morality

SET FOR LIFE

The lobby of the three-room community college is slowly filling with shoes and boots. Chunky skateboard sneakers with wide laces and imitation brown suede boots, knockoffs of an expensive Australian brand, have all been kicked off in the hurry to get to class on time. In the North, it is customary to remove your outdoor shoes so as not to track snow or mud through someone's home or workplace. Some women bring beaded moosehide slippers to wear for the day; young men shuffle about in white tube socks. In the farthest classroom, I wait with Derek, the instructor, for the Introduction to Underground Mining course. It is the first in a sequence of courses meant to help local Indigenous people get jobs in the nearby diamond mines. Derek knows northern Canadian mining industries well. He was a gold miner in the 1990s in Yellowknife. Derek sustained repetitive stress injuries over the course of his career. Overly physical work is now impossible for him. Instead, he flies around the region preparing mining hopefuls to work underground in large, industrial diamond mines.

In 2009, a government and corporate partnership developed courses in underground mining to be delivered in many communities in what was being dubbed Canada's "diamond basin." Derek's class was the inaugural delivery. Trevor and Destiny were enrolled in the course, although neither of them were able to give too many details about it when asked. At the time, two industrial diamond mines were active on the edge of Canada's Arctic. They each had almost exhausted the supply of gemstones that could be harvested using open-pit methods and were supposed to move underground to extend the mines' "lifecycles."[1] A third mine, owned by global diamond conglomerate De Beers, was about to open as the world's first fully underground diamond mine. Corporations and government both promoted the shift in production techniques as an opportunity for local labour, specifically Indigenous labour, to benefit from diamond mining.

Ruth was the first student to arrive. She is fifty and moved to the Northwest Territories over a year ago from Canada's east coast, some 3,700 kilometres away. She heard rumours from a family member that just about anyone with "two hands and a heartbeat" could make $50 an hour working in the mines. Ruth had spent her life running a small catering business that was always floating just above even. The opportunities of the Northern diamond boom seemed worth the trouble to sell everything and move. She started as a cook in one of the mining camps. The shifts were twelve hours a day for two weeks at a time. Staff are flown in and live on site for the duration of their rotations. The pay was only $14/hour. When glossy posters went up around the small Northern town announcing jobs of $100,000 a year, she decided to sign up for the training and change the course of her life. While not a local, Ruth is a registered member of a First Nation in northern New Brunswick and thus her nationally recognized status as Indigenous qualified her for the course. That morning, she wore a jean jacket and had curled her dyed red hair. "I'm guessing there's going to be a lot of young ones in the class," she told me anxiously.

As Destiny, Trevor, and the other trainees arrive, Derek sits on the desk at the front of the room to introduce himself. His teaching uniform is a Harley Davidson T-shirt and faded blue jeans. He begins the class with what he calls "straight talk." "I'm not going to lie," he says, "this course is going to be tough. "But," he hops off the desk, "if you stick with this training, you are looking at a future making one hundred grand a year working in the diamond industry." Ruth shakes

---

1 The industry uses biological metaphors to describe a mine's trajectory to assert some kind of naturalness to a process that is human driven.

her head in disbelief, "If we start making *that* kind of money, we are going to be set for life!"

How do people's hopes for the future become entangled with Arctic mining industries? Each for their own reasons, Destiny, Trevor, and Ruth were hopeful that training for work in the diamond mines would chart their future course for the better. After completing the introductory mining course taught by Derek, they were all scheduled to take a two-week course called Ready for the Job. In line with general transformations of job training programs for the poor and unemployed across North America, Ready for the Job focused on "soft skills" over and above technical industrial know-how (Peck and Theodore 2000; Purser and Hennigan 2017; V. Smith 2010). Soft skills, sometimes called "people skills," have primarily to do with how would-be workers speak and hold their bodies. This chapter focuses on the design and delivery of this particular job readiness program, as its existence was a direct result of efforts to make diamonds ethical by providing training opportunities to Indigenous people. I use the ethnographic description of the training and trainee interpretations of the program to show how competing moral economies are critical elements in Canada's architecture of extraction.

The job training program was, in many respects, an attempt to shape trainees' aspirations for themselves and their futures to align with corporate goals. While it wasn't wholly successful in achieving that level of acculturation, as many trainees resisted the course aims, it nevertheless was successful in normalizing sets of values (like individual responsibility and self-reliance) in ways that were essential to maintaining the ethical value of Canadian diamonds when the 2009 financial crisis hit and none of the promised high-paying jobs materialized.

Anthropologists and other social scientists use the term "moral economy" to bring to light how moral and cultural assumptions about what is good or bad, fair or unjust, right or wrong, are part of any economic institution and/or system (Carrier 2018; Sayer 2000; J.C. Scott 1976; Fischer 2014). Morality and economic activity are inextricably linked. Sometimes this is easy to see, like in the example of consumers who purchase "ethical diamonds" in attempts to have the products they buy reflect their values. There are other moments, however, when it is a little more complicated. Not everyone in an economic system will share the same set of values and moral frameworks. This is especially the case in colonial contexts like Canada, where the economic and moral orders (capitalism, Christianity) have largely been imposed both by force and by more subtle means. Education, whether for children or adults, becomes a prime site of socialization into dominant modes of being. This is why so many Indigenous communities have fought and continue to fight for the right to self-determination with respect to education (L.B. Simpson 2021; Wildcat et al. 2014). As you will see, Ready for the Job attempts to be "culturally sensitive" to Indigenous learners; however, the backbone of the program upholds troubling ideas and explanations as to why many Indigenous people in the Arctic continue to be excluded from the gains of an extractive economy.

The data from this chapter comes out of a unique circumstance tied to my history in the community as a teacher and my experience as a university instructor. After observing the training for the new instructors of Ready for the Job, I was recruited to teach the course after no other instructor was available to travel to Hay River. As I had sat through the instructor training for research purposes, I knew the curriculum well. While I hesitated to accept, I didn't want Ruth, Trevor, Destiny, and the other students to not to have the opportunity to progress through the course sequence. I agreed to be the instructor and then only interviewed the trainees after the course ended.

In the morning before the first class meeting, I sat at my kitchen table preparing the lesson. As I always did, I listened to the radio while I worked. The news that morning was about layoffs at one of the mines. The inaugural delivery of Ready for the Job coincided with the financial crisis of 2008–9. The details of the layoffs made me increasingly anxious about my decision to participate as a course instructor in a program I believed would likely be a dead end for many trainees. As I made my way to the classroom, I decided I didn't want to curb anyone's optimism. I was, however, curious about what these economic shifts might mean for the future of the mining hopefuls whom I had come to know rather well. The readiness program graduation was likely to align with hiring freezes at both operational mines and with stalled plans for the opening of the third mine. I shared my concerns about the hiring freeze the next morning before class.

Trevor folded his arms, balanced his chair on its two back legs and said, "Miss, that doesn't really apply to us. Diamonds are something people will always want. They will always be in demand. Plus, we are from here; they want us in those jobs."

"You ain't from here!" Destiny said, throwing a scrunched-up ball of foolscap paper in Trevor's direction and laughing.

"Well, I'm Aboriginal and that's all they care about," he quipped. Known for liking to push his classmates' buttons, he added, "Plus, I'm Métis which is even better … half white, half Native, best of both worlds!" The class erupted in laughter.

Despite his joking, Trevor had his finger on something that was commonly promoted in local media and everyday talk – namely, that the mines have targets for Northern and Indigenous workers and that they were falling short of meeting those numbers. If Northern hiring targets could not be met, then the multinationals that owned the three mines could easily come under scrutiny. The promise that diamonds are ethical because they are agents of development can't hold if local and Indigenous people don't fill the jobs.

Trevor's comment, "They want us in those jobs," was meant to reinforce a priority relationship with industry based on ethnic citizenship, one that he attempted to include himself in through his comment, "We are from here," and then his correction, "I'm Aboriginal and that's all they care about." We see that he, and other trainees, believe that corporations have a moral obligation to engage Indigenous people as workers. Indeed, they do. This could easily be dismissed as instrumental on their part, however many of the employees I met were extremely sincere in their hopes that access to employment would provide local people with opportunities to achieve "the good life."

Despite intentions, the majority of the trainees I knew did not get work at the end of their training for reasons I will discuss below. Undelivered job promises not only threatened to incite local critique but also stood to interrupt international discourse of Canadian diamonds as ethical commodities. As a reminder, "ethical commodities" accrue value by infusing material objects with moral attributes, which can be assessed by the purchaser or otherwise interested parties (Carrier 2010). Much like commodities that depend on their "authenticity," whether regional or ethnic, for their market value (Cavanaugh and Shankar 2014), ethical commodities are produced through material and linguistic means. Jillian Cavanaugh and Shalini Shankar (2012, 2014) proposed the term "linguistic materiality" to capture the intermingling of material and linguistic labour that aligns or ruptures at various points in the commodity chain. Building on their notion of linguistic materiality, I argue here that ethical commodities not only embody linguistic and material labour, but also exert linguistic and corporeal demands on the kinds of people integral to the idealized commodity story. Semiotic (meaning-making) processes take hold of, and through, people's lives.

In what follows, I outline how and why Indigenous employment, a terrain of competing moral economies, came to participate in the production of diamonds' ethical sign value. According to the training program developers, many people were not accessing work because they lacked the "right attitude."[2] As will become clear, demonstrating the right attitude required that trainees speak in particular ways, what I call "the register of readiness." In outlining the parameters of the register of readiness, I show how the instability of resource economies was turned back onto trainees' individual psychological states when jobs and training funds receded. In sum, job training "failure," refracted through the register of readiness, is essential to producing and maintaining the ethical sign value of Canadian gems by configuring a subset of Indigenous people as "not ready" for work and thus in need of state and industry intervention. If the production of things always involves the production of social relations and subjectivities (Wolf 1982), then the (re)making of the Indigenous underemployed is not a failure of capitalist labour markets but instead an essential component of them.

ALL ABOUT ATTITUDE

When I arrived in Yellowknife to plan the shape of this research, I was struck by how the city had been rebranded as "The Diamond Capital of North America!" Flags announcing this new label hung from most of the downtown lampposts. The visitor's centre had been completely

---

2 Like other studies of job training programs in North America, Ready for the Job's curriculum design reflected larger policy trends that individualize impoverishment and demand the transfiguration of individual subjectivity (Halushka 2016; Purser and Hennigan 2017).

redesigned to showcase the history of diamond development. There were large diorama panels explaining the geological formation of diamonds. There was a collage of photos of smiling faces of local people with text describing their happy relationship to the industry either as employees or as indirect beneficiaries through increased economic activity (e.g., a taxi driver). The abundance of diamond imagery in Yellowknife, coupled with the labour crisis in Canadian mining, meant that I arrived in the Northwest Territories fairly certain that a research project on labour recruitment and training would be easy to execute. I turned up in the capital city of Yellowknife in the summer of 2007 for preliminary work and to establish partnerships with the local training institutions. I began by enquiring about the widely publicized diamond polisher program. As part of the effort to "diversify" the economy, the state made massive investments to help set up a secondary industry in cutting and polishing. At Aurora College, the Territories' only community college, Rick (the director of vocational programs) happily showed me wall charts depicting the cutting and polishing process. Behind a locked door was the delicate equipment. Rick flipped the light switch and I took note of the small wooden benches where would-be workers would sit. "How many people are in the course?" I asked.[3] "None at the moment," he answered. "This course isn't all that popular. We did have some people from Armenia come in and take the class. They finished up last semester. They were really focused. The facilities here are world class. We are thinking about doing more global marketing." This would be the first of a string of disappointments with respect to locating a training program to observe. Part of it was my timing; summer is not generally the time when programs are run. But as I would learn, there was consistent difficulty in obtaining local trainees to fill training spots for several programs. Rumours in local media and everyday talk suggested that despite millions of dollars being put in to training Indigenous workers, few were successful at completing programs or even signing up for them at all.

It was against this backdrop that Ready for the Job was being launched. The program was set to be delivered around the region in various communities to prepare Indigenous trainees for the demands

---

3   The quotations here are not direct. Rather, they are recollections from my field
notes.

of a longer job training program in underground mining. Ready for the Job was developed and mandated as a prerequisite to most vocational training and was aimed at helping to improve program completion rates (in many ways by pushing people out of programs before they begin). The college was generous and allowed me to sit in on the training of course instructors who would soon be sent out to deliver this new two-week course. The course content was not directly related to mining; instead, it was training in what are known as "soft skills." As Urciuoli (2008) has shown, soft skills are primarily commodified communicative acts that align with corporate aims and values. Vocational training seemed like an unlikely place for an emphasis on "soft skills," but when set within the broader context I outline here, we see how and why such a program might emerge.

My training session to become a Ready for the Job instructor opened with a screening of the world's best-selling general employee training video, *FISH!* (ChartHouse Learning, n.d.). It begins with a scene, likely familiar to anyone who has travelled to Seattle's Pike Place Market as a tourist. A huge fish sails through the air and, effortlessly, an employee behind the counter catches the flying fish and wraps it up for a customer, to the delight of a growing audience. "Holy Mackerel!" shouts another employee before launching the next fish to the counter staff. Translated into eighteen languages and sold in thirty-eight countries, The *FISH!* Philosophy is stated simply as "Catch the Energy. Release the Potential." Advertised as boosting employee retention and improving customer relations, *FISH!* has four guiding principles for cultivating effective workplace culture: (1) Play; (2) Make Their Day; (3) Be There;[4] and (4) Choose Your Attitude.

Marilyn, a white woman in her early fifties, was in charge of training instructors to deliver the new curriculum. Marilyn explained that we could use *FISH!* to begin our courses. For her, it was a good teaching tool that addressed the supposed main issue of trainees "from the communities" when it came to successful participation in job training and work placements: attitude. The phrase "from the communities" refers to rural Indigenous settlements scattered around the region, with populations ranging from 200 to 1,000 people. Often, urban

---

4 Refers to "being there" for the customer.

Northerners (Indigenous and not) use the gloss "from the communities" to mean those who are more "traditional," those in need of intervention, or both. It is meant to inscribe cultural difference and distance
between rural have-nots and their urban counterparts. On that first
day of instructor training, Marilyn tapped her long red nails on the
curriculum binder and said, "trainees have to get the right attitude if
they want to be prepared for the reality of the market." "Attitudes"
formed a central component of the Ready for the Job curriculum. The
trainee workbook explained it this way:

> A positive attitude is a state of mind. Individuals with positive atti-
> tudes approach activities and people with expectations of positive
> outcomes. This optimism motivates them to work hard within their
> families, schools, jobs, and communities.... People with positive atti-
> tudes do not blame others for problems. They think about a situation,
> determine what is within their control and authority, and then decide
> what actions to take. (Government of Northwest Territories 2006, 7)

This excerpt individualizes trainees' emotional states and psychological compositions (Haney 2010, 14). It places the "problem of attitude"
squarely in the minds of trainees. If we understand Michel Foucault's
governance to be the patterns of power and regulation that shape,
guide, and manage social conduct, then we can begin to see that job
training is a form of state regulation based on incursions into people's individual psyches. Sharing many similarities to the discourses
described in ethnographies of North American clinical spaces directed
at the poor (Carr 2010; Haney 2010), Northern training discourse mo-
bilizes a strikingly therapeutic, self-help lexicon. To be prepared for
"the reality of the market," would-be workers needed to adjust their
individual psychological states. Ready for the Job included personality tests, learning-style inventories, and communication-style quizzes
that all aimed to provide trainees with acceptable ways of knowing
and expressing themselves. Curricular activities were designed to help
trainees access their "true" interior states and then relay that information through talk about themselves to trainers and eventually to prospective employers. For example, trainees spent half a day using True
Colors International's personality assessment tools. As the company's
website explains, "the True Colors proprietary system distills complex

temperament theory into practical tools and actionable programs. We use colors – Orange, Gold, Green, and Blue – to differentiate the four central primary personality types" (True Colors International, n.d.). Trainees were guided through a process to determine which of the four colours they were. Self-visions required that trainees narrate themselves as individual, autonomous, and ultimately free of any explicit assessments of the social world that conflicted with the training staff's. Conflicts could be resolved by understanding other people's "true colors" and managed by simply identifying the two different personal temperaments at play (e.g., "I am a blue and she is an orange. I am likely being too sensitive!"). Part of the program was to help trainees see themselves, and thus speak about themselves, differently. Trainees needed new visions (or, likely, versions) of themselves if they wanted to be "set for life." The assumption here is that Indigenous people do not know about themselves, nor how to talk about their "potential." Said differently, they are unable to prioritize their capacities as labour in everyday speech acts.

After screening the *FISH!* video, Marilyn zeroed in on the relationship between "positive attitude" and "taking responsibility." She told us that a major issue was that people from the communities needed "to stop blaming others for their problems." Placing blame, here, is understood as having a false understanding of who is responsible for a situation. With a strong individualizing ethos, I would later observe staff reminding trainees again and again that "they needed to be responsible for their actions." Blaming was seen as a sign that trainees were not yet able or willing to see the situation as a result of *their own* actions. It was a reflection of not only the wrong reasoning, but of the wrong state of mind.

Poor attitudes, defined largely as "blaming" or "not taking responsibility," were understood as signs of a failure to produce the proper state of mind. It was this improper state of mind, then, that was used to explain why more Indigenous workers were not climbing the ranks of a high-paying industry like mining. Carr's (2010) study of a state-funded women's addiction treatment centre in the midwestern United States highlights the dangers of casting political and economic issues of poverty and homelessness as essentially therapeutic concerns. As will become clear over the course of this chapter, her warnings should be heeded for Indigenous underemployment and unemployment.

The correlation between "taking responsibility" and "not blaming" is important to look at closely in the context of a training program directed at Indigenous workers. With many outstanding legal and political battles between Indigenous collectives and the state regarding historical – and enduring – inequalities (such as residential schooling, land seizure), there is a public sentiment that Indigenous people are "blaming" the government for things that happened long ago. There are often remarks among Northerners, and even among some Indigenous residents, that Indigenous people need to simply "get over it" or "just move on." The linking of "blaming" to the acquisition or maintenance of "special rights" for Indigenous people is part of that tension.

If attitude is a "state of mind," how can external agents like trainers and employers assess it? The training manual focused on shaping behaviours and ways of speaking, which would communicate the "right attitude." Without these externally legible forms of "attitude," it was to be assumed that trainees did not have the right "state of mind." To display a "positive attitude" was to speak in what I call a "register of responsibility." While trainers often tried to shape the ways trainees were thinking (about themselves or their situations), what they were actually shaping was a way of speaking. I use the term "register of responsibility" to bring together a set of linguistic and embodied practices that were used to assess individuals as having (or not) "the right attitude" and as "being responsible." States of mind were in fact states of talk.

REGISTER OF READINESS

What do I mean by the term "register of readiness"? Asif Agha (2004, 24) defines a register as "a linguistic repertoire that is associated, culture-internally, with particular social practices and with persons who engage in such practices" (see also Agha 2005, 2011). The focus on "soft skills" meant that students were learning to speak about themselves in particular ways to demonstrate their positive attitudes and thus their "readiness" for work. Like the job readiness initiatives described by Emily Cummins and Linda Blum (2015), the register of readiness focused on instilling racialized, classed body norms. Four multimodal linguistic features defined the register of readiness. First, the course encouraged a high degree of self-referential talk that prioritized the speaker as agent (denoted by using primarily first-person constructions). For example, trainees were asked to speak using "I statements" (e.g., "I am very frustrated with the assignment," not "The assignment is frustrating").

Second, the register of readiness asked that workers' bodily habits align with employer expectations for deference; making eye contact while speaking and being sure not to cross one's arms were both described as open communication strategies. Women were taught to be sure to cover their "three Bs" (backs, breasts, and buttocks). Bodily comportment was to be monitored and regulated. Marilyn warned us that "the young guys like to wear their pants low and pull their hats over their eyes." It was our job to enforce a "no hat" policy and to make sure the young men understood that these things made them "unapproachable." Other stated rules included not having underwear showing, no feet shuffling, no cracking knuckles, no hooded or oversized clothing: many of the very things crucial to contemporary working-class Indigenous identity, with elements borrowed from hip-hop culture. While the curriculum cheerfully exploited certain cultural norms, it blatantly outlawed others. For example, the adage "respect your elders" was used strategically to teach trainees to listen to their superiors, an already sanctioned cultural practice.

Third, the register of readiness emphasized expressions of desired independence. Trainees were reminded that they needed to "help themselves before they help others." Family ties that were too tight were seen as infringing on success in the workplace. Independence largely referred to financial independence. Later, I would watch as Derek (the Introduction to Mining instructor) attempted to cultivate trainees' "need" for independence in positive, not punitive, terms. At the outset of the course, Derek sat up on his desk at the front of the small classroom and asked the trainees to "imagine walking into a bike shop, or a snow machine shop, or whatever. Imagine walking in and paying cash for what you want. Just straight out buying it. Now that is freedom." Statements that revealed that trainees relied on others for income, or were sharing income, were ill regarded by training staff.

Finally, the register of readiness was characterized by positive self-assessments expressed in extended turns at talk. Because curriculum interventions targeted what was perceived to be the root cause of "bad attitudes," namely "low self-esteem," or an inaccurate understanding of the self, trainees needed to speak positively, and at length about their accomplishments. The register of readiness carries with it ideas about the very nature of language itself. In other words, it emphasizes a particular language ideology. The two defining ideological features of the register of readiness are: (1) speech is simply referential; and (2) talk is a direct reflection of mental states or individual intention, or what E. Summerson Carr terms an ideology of inner reference. The ideology of inner reference presumes that, first, "healthy" language refers to pre-existing phenomena and, second, that the phenomena to which it refers are internal to speakers (Carr 2010, 4). In my case, "a positive attitude" was a phenomenon that was not necessarily pre-existing but was understood as always possible or immanent.[5] Possible positive attitudes were assumed to be inherent in speakers. What matters for the exploration of diamonds-turned-ethical commodities is that the promotion of "readiness talk," rather than being a neutral employment skill, became crucial to the management of the impermanence of resource extraction. But how did the implementation of the program work? Did trainees readily adopt the "register of readiness"? I would soon find out. At the end of the instructor training, I was caught off guard when I was asked to teach Ready for the Job in Hay River. I wondered how I would – or if I even could – carry out a program that I had considerable objections to. At the same time, I knew that participating in this way meant a different type of access to the institutional side of the program. I accepted and quickly set about making a few changes to the syllabus: complementing the unit on having a positive attitude with Marx's theory of surplus value and swapping the workplace responsibilities section with workplace rights.

LIGHTS KNOCKED OUT

Once into the course, it became obvious that trainees had difficulty with some aspects of the register of readiness. On one of our first days

---

5 Encouraging positivity, optimism, and a general self-help ethos is not uncommon in programming for North American underclasses. The increasing hybridization of self-help and formal modes of social service in the United States is documented by Fairbanks (2009), Goode and Maskovsky (2002), and Carr (2010).

together, I led trainees through a role-playing exercise on "providing quality customer service." The exercise asked trainees to affirm the imagined customer's needs by using an "I statement" and the customer's name. In the provided scenario, a customer in an auto body shop is upset about her bill. In response, trainees are encouraged to say something like, "I would be happy to give you a breakdown of those costs, Susan." During the class discussion that followed the role play, Richard, a Métis man in his forties with decades of industry experience, shook his head in disbelief, "If you talk like *that* on a job site, you'll get your lights knocked out!" Richard's comment points out that the promoted performance of soft skills is at odds with workplace norms. Richard's comment and general frustration with course materials revealed the ways in which corporate values were not in line with corporeal norms of a highly masculinized sector. Many trainees recognized the register of readiness as irrelevant to entry-level industrial work. Moreover, they experienced therapeutic, self-help talk as boasting, which was foreign and uncomfortable for them. As Ruth put it, "So you mean, we are supposed to brag about ourselves?" While the training staff believed that the register of readiness indexed speakers who were ready for the job, trainees understood it differently. The process by which a linguistic repertoire comes to be associated with particular social practices and with persons who engage in such practices is known as enregisterment (Agha 2004). With the majority of educators and managers being non-Indigenous, these habits of speaking and being have come to be enregistered as white. Once the course ended, Destiny told me, "I'm not gonna fucking talk white! I don't want to be all like, 'Hi there! How can I help you?!'" she said in mock valley-girl speech.

For many trainees, the register of readiness was at odds with their sense of self and local linguistic norms, putting many people in a double bind when it came to accessing work and social assistance. When I asked what they felt they needed to get one of the coveted mine jobs, the trainees showed highly sophisticated "metalinguistic awareness" (Cazden 1974). Metalinguistic awareness refers to the ability to reflect consciously on the nature of language and the social functions it carries out. For example, trainees knew that employers favoured certain ways of talking. Their job, as they saw it, was to learn not only technical mining facts but also how to present themselves in the right way to potential employers. When I asked the trainees what would be most helpful for the course's focus, everyone agreed – "interview practice!" Ruth, who spoke with speech features characteristic of working-class people from the Maritime provinces, explained, "We's can get alls [*sic*] the training we want, but when we open our mouths, they're gonna think we are uneducated." Scott, an Inuit man in his forties, felt he "wasn't great at talking about [himself]." He was not alone. Most trainees disliked the idea that they had to speak about themselves. Despite these tensions around what linguistic habits could and should be cultivated, everyone was keen on passing the standardized Ready for the Job exam. Passing would allow trainees to move onto a twelve-week simulated mine camp training experience with people from all over the NWT. They would live in a former addiction treatment centre turned conference centre far from their home communities to simulate mine work life conditions. There would be three meals a day, strict behaviour codes, and a security guard stationed at the front to ensure they did not head into town. The more immediate reward that trainees were looking forward to was a promised "fancy dinner" for passing Ready for the Job. One restaurant in town is markedly more expensive than the others, and many trainees had never eaten there; the possibility of going generated a fair bit of excitement.

GRADUATION HAT

As the trainees worked through their course, the financial crisis started to affect the mining industry, and the diamond mines began layoffs. Two days before their exam, a cardboard box arrived at the college. Inside were graduation certificates and baseball caps with the training agency's logo. As I was the impromptu teacher, I called the head office in Yellowknife to sort out the details of the dinner. The agency decided to replace the fancy dinner with the more cost-effective hat. The agency secretary sympathetically reassured me that this was "no big deal" because "those who are *selected* for the next stage of the course … will get a full graduation ceremony and eventually be making $100,000 a year."

The news that only selected trainees would move on came to me as a surprise. The trainees all shared my impression that if they passed the two courses, then they automatically qualified for the full certificate program once they proved they were officially "ready for the job." Because the industry was hesitant to renew funding, the agency faced declining resources and was not sure what it could afford for the upcoming course. The dwindling funds and the insecurity it caused were ultimately downloaded onto the trainees. Through a long and drawn-out period, the agency tried to assess its financial situation. During this time, the trainees were unable to claim any social assistance or seek work, as they could be called to the next stage of the program at any time. When I communicated to the trainees that not all of them who passed would move on to the next phase, I felt the classroom dynamics shift almost immediately. Some trainees harnessed the language of individual responsibility to make themselves more marketable. Their shared fight to pass the courses was now a competition. For some, this meant constructing their classmates as "not really serious."

The personal stakes for trainees were high. Trevor had been put on early parole to attend classes and his release was conditional on enrolment. Destiny's housing subsidy was attached to school enrolment. While I was never sure she dreamed of being a miner, I am certain she longed for stable housing. After three months, although all six trainees passed the standardized exam, only four were selected to go to Yellowknife. Destiny and Trevor were pushed out.[6] Trevor moved back to Saskatchewan and eventually landed a job in Alberta's oil sands driving heavy equipment. Since the training in 2008–9, he has become the proud father of twin girls and does two-week rotations between home and work. In the next chapter, I will explain what happened to Destiny when she lost her housing and "took off" to reconnect with an old flame living on a reservation some 312 kilometres away.

The four successful trainees were to receive financial assistance to cover costs of the next training, with the exception of Ruth. Although Indigenous, she is from New Brunswick and thus did not qualify for assistance. She had to take out a personal loan at a high interest rate to cover her costs. She and her husband decided it was worth the investment to get a coveted "hundred grand" job at the program's end.

---

6 I can't say for certain why these two were not selected, but my guess is that they were two of the youngest and most assertive trainees.

In a month's time, the four trainees would pack up and move around the lake to live in the simulated mine camp. I visited the successful trainees "in camp" twice during their twelve-week training, which included both positive things, such as three cooked meals a day and a comfortable place to stay, and negative things, such as strict curfews, a lengthy list of rules that included no alcohol, and a security guard who tracked their comings and goings.

During the in-camp phase, the larger group of twenty-eight trainees from around the NWT gelled into a cohort. At one point, trainees "flipped the script" (Carr 2010) of readiness on the agency staff. According to the trainees, the agency staff never followed their own rules or made good on their commitments. They were frequently late and made promises they did not keep. Previous let-downs (the cancelled graduation dinner, funding changes) became evidence that the staff were themselves "not responsible." Trainees noticed the start times of meetings with staff diligently, and Ruth, who had taken charge of the mounting complaints, rigorously recorded any staff lateness. Towards the end of the program, trainees were scheduled to meet with agency staff to go over the final exam schedule. After thirty minutes of waiting with no sign of the staff, they decided to stage a lockout: they lured the security guard away from the front desk and bolted the front door. They said if they were not allowed to be more than fifteen minutes late, then the staff members should not be allowed either.

These acts of resistance formed intense bonds of solidarity. However, it is easy to see the limitations of such resistance in making significant change. The everyday battles that the trainees had with the staff ultimately missed their targets. The problem was that the trainees had begun to think of staff as "irresponsible individuals" instead of questioning larger structural problems that affected resource extraction work. In using the curriculum-sanctioned register of readiness, trainee critiques were largely apolitical. Promoted forms of talk directed trainee attention inward. In this way, standards of readiness – such as being on time, keeping promises, or being transparent – could not be measured against the staff. While a register of readiness provided a channel for trainee concerns to be voiced, prioritizing talk that can only reference inner states meant that trainee concerns could easily be dismissed as "blaming." The adoption of certain metanarratives of the self was tied to the allocation of resources (to be kept in the program, to be promoted through the phases, or not kept or promoted), and therefore stakes were high for mastering rituals of speaking and communication.

Throughout the underground mining program, trainees were repeatedly told that mine employers would be hiring at their graduation. After completing the full training program, many had, as instructed, come with their polished résumés in hand in the event that they were hired on the spot and thus "set for life." A level of disorganization that was standard to the program marked the graduation ceremony. Trainees were having their photos taken out front while staff scrambled to organize the details of the barbecue that was supposed to follow. When the trainees came in and took their seats, a few key personnel had not yet arrived, although it was fifteen minutes past the start time. Tiffany, the master of ceremonies and an agency staff member, came up to announce that they would be starting shortly and that the event was running on "Indian time." Despite the fact that the twenty-six "Indians" who had not missed a single minute of class time were all seated directly in front of her and that the two missing personnel were not from the Northwest Territories, the comment still got a few light laughs from the guests.

Only one representative from a mine was present at the graduation. He congratulated the group and talked of the "downturn" and said it was an "opportunity to exercise patience and flexibility." He estimated that hiring would begin again in six months and encouraged them to keep "getting out of bed every morning" and to "stay on the right track." With those words, I watched Ruth roll up her printed résumés and stuff them in her purse. Her husband, who had travelled 250 miles to the ceremony, reached for her hand.

Tiffany returned to the front and closed by telling the trainees, "The most difficult chains to break are the ones inside of us." "Don't be a victim of circumstance," she warned. Her words echoed what I heard elsewhere about the ascription of contemporary issues as "internal," though they might be more aptly linked to poverty and legacies of colonialism. This closing remark – and the event as a whole – illustrates how structural deficiencies of social programming through resource work can be turned into personal battles that responsible individuals need to face. After a year, none of the trainees had one of the promised $100,000-per-year jobs. In fact, only one got a related job at all.

In the context of resource-dependent regions like the diamond basin, the promotion of "readiness talk" is far from a neutral employment skill. It is crucial to the management of the impermanence of resource extraction. By promoting types of talk that eschew trainee critique and concerns, the instability of resource economies is turned back onto trainees' psychological states. Moralizing dimensions of classroom text and talk in this specific context remap structural instabilities of resource development onto individual and household aspirations for "the good life." As it turned out, there was not a pot of gold at the end of the rainbow. There were no jobs available to the trainees on graduation day. Agency staff naturalized this as "the cycle" of the market, and trainees' newly developed soft skills of patience and flexibility were called on to weather the storm.

My aim here has been to outline locally situated meanings and consequences of the register of readiness. The malleability of soft skills as a conceptual apparatus lends itself to existing ideas about language, culture, ethnicity, and morality. The exclusion of some citizens from national narratives of "the good life" is easily reframed as a question of attitude. Educational ideologies like the "skills gap" and "getting the right attitude" eventually come to both explain and attempt to solve the co-presence of mineral wealth and the uneven distribution of everyday difficulties in Canada's North. Security guards, curfews, punitive attendance, and cash payments (which were unreliable and dwindled) were forms of governance intended to guide and manage conduct but also to orient individuals to the job market. Any failures were deemed personal. Ready for the Job aimed to have trainees become conversant in the language of individual responsibility. But did trainees simply become governable subjects? The answer is largely no. Only the trainees who already possessed some of the values and behaviours favoured by Ready for the Job showed up to and stuck with the course. In this way, Ready for the Job did not create governable subjects; it simply located and identified them as such. "Successful" trainees had strong histories with wage work, and their values aligned with those of potential employers more closely than their "unsuccessful" counterparts. This was not because of their training; these differences were largely pre-existing. As a result, these existing local class differences were reinscribed. This conclusion underscores the importance of adopting an approach to resource politics that attends to the class trajectories of Indigenous people in North America (Dombrowski 2001; Sider 2003b) or other parts of the world (T. Li 2010; Steur 2014).

CONCLUSION

The marketing of diamonds from Canada not only involves creating physical and racial distance from "African" problems (Falls 2011, 2014; Ferguson 2006; Le Billon 2006, 2008) but also stresses industry's capacity to improve life for people who are seen to be on the margins of the nation, both geographically and socio-economically. Northern Canada is home to diverse Indigenous peoples (Dene, Inuvialuit, Inuit, and Métis) who, when compared to their non-Indigenous counterparts, endure higher rates of social harm and homelessness (Christensen 2016). At the height of the diamond boom, diamonds were promoted by state and industry as development agents, offering Canada's Indigenous people access to high-wage work and training opportunities. Promises of work and improved standards of living were directed not only towards communities but to consumers as well. For example, Brilliant Earth (n.d.-a, n.d.-b), North America's largest purveyor of finished "ethical" jewellery, describes stones from Canada as going "beyond conflict-free" as "mines have demonstrated a strong commitment to hiring local Aboriginal people, providing a skilled apprenticeship program and improving the average income and unemployment rate." In this way, potential mine work was not only a matter of configuring individual future aspirations but was essential in positioning select diamonds as ethical at a time when the gemstones' capacity to signify love was undermined by global blood diamonds campaigns.

Economic systems aggressively promote moral values (Fischer 2014). By attending to curriculum design and classroom talk, I illustrated how a register of readiness, assumed by curriculum designers to be an index of individuals' preparedness for the demanding work cycle of an underground miner, was for trainees at odds with how they understood themselves and their experiences as workers. It was an attempt to acculturate them into a way of speaking but also into a moral framework for being. For them, many features of the register of readiness were associated with femininity or whiteness, often both. More important than mismatched interpretations of a speech style, the register of readiness emphasized inward investigation over social critique and thus became crucial in managing the impermanence of resource extraction. Registers of readiness trivialized trainee critique and concerns about the structural problems associated with resource work. In the process, the instability of resource economies was ultimately turned back onto trainees' psychological states. Said plainly, trainee critiques were evaluated as "blaming" and disappeared job opportunities were reframed as "opportunities to exercise patience."

Soft skills have been evaluated critically by social scientists as a broad and amorphous group of personal characteristics that includes things like attitudes towards work, flexibility, and character.[7] Under the banner of neoliberalism, many have been quick to point out that the turn to soft skills emphasizes self-transformation over structural change (Cremin 2010; Hughes 2005; Purser and Hennigan 2017). Here I connect critical evaluations of soft skills to anthropological work concerned with ethical commodities on the one hand (Berlan 2012; Besky 2013; Carrier 2010; Grasseni 2013) and the social life of corporate (mining) forms on the other (Golub 2014; Kirsch 2014; F. Li 2009, 2011; Rajak 2011; Welker 2014; Welker, Partridge, and Hardin 2011). I showed how semiotic work to produce "ethical" brands is linked to face-to-face interactions, not only among workers and corporate representatives, sellers, and consumers, but also among those on whose behalf ethical development plans are made. What I want to underscore here is that the promotion of soft skills in the context of mining hard rocks cannot fully be understood as merely a poor attempt to produce ideal workers, although it is that too. Diamonds from Canada, marketed as ethical commodities, require would-be workers as much as they need labourers in the pits. The underemployed are crucial to the promotion of diamonds as development. The struggle to try and reconcile competing moral economies (e.g., discouraging Indigenous grandparents from sharing money with trainees) actually comes

---

7 Many scholars have contextualized the importance of soft skills in the "new economy" with service work placing new value on workers' linguistic capacities (Cameron 2000; Cavanaugh and Shankar 2014; Duchêne and Heller 2012; Heller et al. 2015; McLaughlin 2013, 2015; Sonntag 2005).

to be a key element in the architecture of extraction. The register of readiness, and the moral framework it presupposes, mediates the contradiction of unpredictable job promises by recasting dried-up opportunities as "opportunities to exercise patience" and thereby thwarts trainee critique and maintains the brand reputation of Canadian diamonds locally and globally. And while mining does not make jobs for those on the margins, for those with resource entangled futures, it does contain a possibility that things might be different – that one day we might be "set for life."

DISCUSSION QUESTIONS

1 What does a typical university/college classroom look like at your institution? What cultural values are implied/enforced by the spatial organization of the room?
2 The author describes the job training program as "a terrain of competing moral economies." In your own words, what does this mean?
3 Even if you are not multi-lingual, you likely shift registers in the course of a given week. What communities or environments that you participate in have distinct registers? What are some of the traits of that register?
4 Describe some of the qualities of the "register of readiness." Is your own way of speaking close to or far from this way of speaking? Why or why not might that be the case?
5 How does the desire to have "ethical" diamonds shape everyday life for the under- and unemployed in this community?

CHAPTER SEVEN

Aspiration

In January 2009, the NWT's diamond mines went into "maintenance mode," meaning production stopped to control the supply of stones to market and reduce labour costs. Forecasted plans for new mines were put on hold. Training funds were reduced. When retracted program funding essentially pushed Destiny out of the job program described in the last chapter, she did not dwell on her unfulfilled career as a miner. Destiny's major concern was housing. She was receiving a subsidy from the territorial government for being in school. No schooling meant no housing. Knowing her housing was in jeopardy, I asked her what she planned to do. Flipping up the hood of her sweatshirt, she said, "I'm thinking about taking off." The next day Destiny stood on the side of the only paved highway leading out of the NWT. She waited until someone heading south picked her up. She crossed the sixtieth parallel and kept on "catching rides" until she reached the nearest urban centre, Edmonton, Alberta, about 1,000 kilometres away.

Seven weeks after Destiny "took off" in the midst of the financial crisis, she returned to Hay River pregnant and with bruises scattered across her body. I picked her up from the bus depot, relieved to see her but worried about what she had gone through. I also felt angry that the instability of resource work was downloaded to individual Indigenous women in a way that could not easily be pointed to as systematic but was not simply coincidental. My outrage didn't align with Destiny's interpretations of herself or the situation. While I wanted to be angry at institutions and structures, she seemed puzzled by my emotions and explanations. She didn't want to lament the past. She wanted to talk about her future as a mother. This future continued to involve resource extraction in complicated ways.

Every promised opening of a mine comes with a sense of its closure. Contemporary mining projects make their impermanence very clear to local communities. Even corporations' overly generous estimates of a mine's "lifecycle" still contain closure dates and plans. How then do people begin to think about a stable future in the context of this forecasted impermanence? What do people expect from extraction? These questions, along with Destiny's continued entanglement with a resource-laden future, forced me to see aspiration as a critical element in Canada's architecture of extraction.

In the last chapter, I showed how job training programs attempted to reroute local moral economies towards ideas and ideals more congruent with wage work, private property, and extractive capital. Part of this involved homing in on and shaping trainees' aspirations for themselves and their futures and what exactly constituted "the good life." In this chapter, I narrow in on Indigenous women's varied natural resource–related aspirations. By aspiration, I mean "a hope for the future informed by ideas about the good life [that] gives direction to agency – the power to act and have a sense of control over one's destiny" (Fischer 2014, 207).

This chapter revolves around two groups of women – working-class Indigenous women, like Destiny, and middle-class Métis women. All these women have varied ways of making resource-entangled futures. While mining is often assumed to be the domain of men, and indeed men make up the bulk of the direct workforce, part of what I show here is how women's household contributions and aspirations are key driving forces in how northern Canada's economy works. Taken together, their stories illustrate how aspirations vary along lines of race, citizenship, and class – and these differentiated aspirations are central to, not by-products of, extraction. Diverse, gendered, and racialized forms of aspiring are the final critical element in the Arctic's architecture of extraction.

FROM AFFECT TO ASPIRATION

Questions about how people in mining contexts think about the future are of interest not merely to social science, but also to states and mining companies as well. These latter entities increasingly, and self-consciously, attempt to manage or prevent community protest by channelling expectations and affects through juro-political techniques, like community consultations (Weszkalnys 2016). Such practices make clear how workers' ideas about the future, and public feelings about extractive activity more generally, are not external to economic activity but rather essential to it. As Weszkalnys (2016, 128) describes in the case of oil, such public sentiments "give economies their specific shape, while also being shaped by them." Diamonds, like all natural resources, are not simply abstract commodities, but are "entangled in the affective fabric of contemporary economic life" (Weszkalnys 2016, 127; see also Ferry and Limbert 2008). In reflecting on Destiny's lack of anger at industry, as well as the transformation of the NWT from having a strong base of anti-extractive activists in the 1960s to having large-scale diamond mines operate with little opposition in the 2000s, I was reminded of a quote by anthropologist William Mazzarella (2010). He writes that "[a]ny social project that is not imposed through force alone must be affective in order to be effective" (299). What I learned from my time in the field was that elements of extractive economies must resonate with people's aspirations for the future or else they would not proceed.

Recently, anthropologists of resource extraction have turned towards the concept of "affect" to grapple with the emergent relationship between human and non-human materialities. Part of a broader "affective turn" in the social sciences and humanities that grew in the late 1990s, researchers and theorists began to consider alternative ways of understanding human experience. The term "affect" offers a way of signalling sentiments that are at once personal yet public, emergent yet orienting. Affect is often associated with Raymond Williams's term "structures of feeling," which was intended to describe what he called "social experiences in solution." Williams, a Marxist theorist, was trying to show how particular modes of production were tied to sentiments that weren't always clearly articulate-able but nevertheless capable of exerting a force on people's lives. As a term, "structures of feeling" tried to capture how some social experiences do not need definition, classification, or rationalization before they have felt effects or exert palpable pressures (Williams 1977, 132–3). In my years living in semi-urban Northern locales, the extractive industry around Arctic natural resources had affective resonances/met these criteria. While a select group of "community representatives" consulted with corporations and other researchers countless times to discuss the future of diamond mining in the NWT, most people had little to say directly on the matter. Nevertheless, the possibility of increased extraction exerted a social force on how people thought about their futures. It did for Bonnie, Ruth, and Destiny – and I can say it certainly did for me. My initial arrival in the North was very much built on my own middle-class aspirations as someone who came from a family that was highly class anxious. I could relate deeply with other white women I met who had moved north in search of middle-class security. This security, even if indirectly, is afforded by an economy based on extractive industry.

While affect is a critical component to understanding the social and political dimensions of Arctic extraction, it presents a set of methodological problems. Affect is described as a "domain of intensity" (Massumi 2002) and an "element of experience that comes before the determination of subject and sense" (Rajchman 2001, 15). From this vantage, affect precedes "narrativizable action-reaction circuits" (Massumi 2002, 28; Mazzarella 2010, 292) or is that which can be felt but not talked about clearly just yet. Attention to affect is at once phenomenological and historical. As Mazzarella (2010, 292) explains, "From the standpoint of affect, society is inscribed on our nervous system and in our flesh before it appears in our consciousness. The affective body is by no means a tabula rasa; it preserves the traces of past actions and encounters and brings them into the present as potentials." This means that typical ethnographic modes of data gathering and representation (soliciting narrative, writing narrative) are ill-suited to the task of attending to affect. As Mazzarella (2010, 293) remarks, "Conventional social analysis is always arriving too late to the scene of a crime it is incapable of recognizing: culture has already done its covering work." Therefore, to solicit through interviews "resource affects" and then name them as such, subjects embodied experiences to semiotic and semantic processes that try to contain them. Here, I opt for a focus on aspiration over affect to allow me to lean on the explicit ways in which women in the community talked about their futures and how mining did – or did not – figure into those futures.

TIGHTLY ENTANGLED

In northern Canada, Indigenous, working-class women's futures are tightly entangled with extractive industry – however, not in uniform ways. Destiny and Ruth's stories show how this entanglement takes both more and less direct forms. Ruth, whom I discussed in the last chapter, is a fifty-year-old Indigenous woman who moved from Canada's east coast hoping to be "set for life" through work in the mines. The end of Destiny and Ruth's training course coincided with the timeline of the global financial crisis reaching the sixtieth parallel. At the end of the training program, Destiny "took off" to deal with her lack of housing. As a prospective mine worker, her history of "taking off" made Destiny a "bad investment" in the eyes of the program and its funders, namely industry, the state, and her Indigenous band. In *The Souls of Black Folk* (1903, 1), W.E.B. DuBois asked, "How does it feel to be a problem?" Later, writing about South Asians as "model minorities" in the US, Vijay Prashad (2000, 6), in *The Karma of Brown Folk,* asked, "How does it feel to be a solution?" Inverting the question one more time in the wake of the 2009 financial crisis, Lauren Berlant offered this question about foreclosed homeowners, "How does it feel to be a bad investment?" In Canada, Indigenous people, far more than working-class settler populations, are discussed as resources with capacity to generate returns on investments in and for a national future. What became clear to me in listening to Destiny talk about her life was that she never experienced herself as a bad investment, even if the job training staff did. In "taking off" Destiny feels herself a strong, independent Dene woman. Like many women her age, her future aspirations revolved around romantic partnering and financial stability.

Eventually, Destiny gave birth to a baby girl who she named Nevaeh. "It's heaven spelled backwards," she told me. By the time Nevaeh was born, I was back in Toronto writing my dissertation. Destiny called me when Nevaeh was two months old because she was unsure about whether to register Nevaeh with her own Indigenous band in Hay River or to cross over into oil-rich Alberta and have the baby registered with the baby's father's band. In Canada, Indigenous children must be registered with an Indigenous group to be a member and, in turn, receive any benefits associated with membership. When parents are from two different groups, the parents can decide on the baby's registration. Destiny wanted to know which band I thought had more possibilities in terms of new resources prospects in the region. New projects hold the potential of revenue streams for band members. If new projects are approved, sometimes royalty payments are shared with group members. In Alberta, the groups closest to the most active oil fields are often presumed to be wealthy; however, the economic benefits of these mega-projects are uneven at best; they have been called "slow industrial genocide" and have been heavily criticized (Huseman and Short 2012; Parson and Ray 2018; Preston 2017). Destiny saw it differently. "I just want my daughter to have a good future." Even if diamonds aren't forever, Destiny's expectations for tomorrow are caught up with the ongoing possibility of extraction and the possibilities it creates. In this way, her ambitions express a much longer process than the single-project model proposed by the state and industry. As she looks to the future, she tries to imagine which regions may prove to be resource rich, as they will provide much-needed income to sustain her and her new family. I learned in our conversations that some of her aspirations cohere around the idea of extraction as ongoing, endless, and generative of resources for her and her family. Even if those looking at it from the outside may see this as an unfounded and a risky outlook, it is a worthwhile imaginary to describe. Her aspirations run counter to outsider academic arguments about "slow industrial genocide," at least in terms of everyday experience.

Aspirations are limited by what Fischer (2014, 6) calls opportunity structures, which are "social norms, legal regulations, and market entry mechanisms that delimit, or facilitate, certain behaviors or aspirations." Destiny's aspirations are invariably shaped by the opportunity structures that arise from the processes and histories I have described so far. My aim isn't just to accept her aspirations at face value as a way to say, "Industry is good and local people depend on it." Instead, I want to show how no other paths forward seemed as viable to her. Unlike me and other privileged Canadians, Destiny has very few other options than to tie herself and her family's future to an industry that is notoriously unpredictable and violent (environmentally, culturally, and otherwise).

Indigenous working-class women are not a homogenous group. For many, their future expectations are bound up with extraction in the most explicit ways when compared to others in the community, but not in precisely the same ways. This becomes clear when we return to Ruth's story. A month after the mining course ended, Ruth called and asked if I could help her apply online for a job. She heard one of the mines was hiring and was having a hard time navigating their website. She also wanted to send out resumes and cover letters to a few other leads in transportation. At the community college, we sat in front of the computer and worked together on "selling" Ruth's new skills. As we reread our draft of her cover letter, it occurred to me that something may be missing. The following conversation ensued:

L: Do you want to say you are an Aboriginal woman in the letter?

R: Why would I do that? Do you think I should?

L: Hmmm. Well, technically they are supposed to give priority hires to Aboriginals and Northerners.

R: Yeah, but I am not from here.

L: Right, but you have lived here for three years, so that makes you a Northerner.

R: Ok, so I should say I am a Northerner. But, I mean, I AM Aboriginal. Is that better?

L: I don't know. I have been trying to figure out how these categories work for the past year.

R: I just don't want to make some big deal out of it. It might look like I am trouble, you know, demanding. What do you think?

L: It's up to you. We could say that a copy of your license and Indian Status Card are available upon request. That way they would know, but you wouldn't be making it, like, a big deal. I just know that contractors get more "points" if they have Northern and Aboriginal employees. More points means they have a better chance of winning bids. I wouldn't want you to miss out if it really is an advantage. But, like I said, I don't know.

R: Let's put it as the upon request, then it's there without really being there. (Field notes, September 7, 2009)

In our conversation, it was clear that both Ruth and I understood the links between categories of race and citizenship and extractive industry as ambiguous at best. While Ruth was persistent in her belief that mining would make her "set for life," the ways in which that related to her Indigeneity was unclear. On the one hand, she was aware of stereotypes that being "too" Indigenous could signal non-deference to largely settler employers; on the other hand, she was aware of the political-legal landscape in which mines had been approved under the guise that they provide local, specifically Indigenous, employment. After a little more editing, we sent off Ruth's packages. I checked in with her a month later. She had had no responses and was considering going back into catering. Her persistence (and her husband's income) meant that Ruth could hold out for the hiring freeze to end. After about seven months, she got a job in one of the mines and has now worked in the diamond mines for nearly ten years. Her initial comments about the working conditions were highly positive. Like many employees, she talked about the camp amenities and the occasional exciting menu items like lobster. Her most recent posts on social media, however, suggest exhaustion has set in. The high salaries are proving to be insufficient due to high costs of living in Hay River. With friends and family on Facebook, she debates packing it all in and going home to the east coast.

Ruth's aspirations hinge more on access to wage work than Destiny's. This makes sense as Ruth is Indigenous but non-local, and therefore she is excluded from any other revenue sharing that could happen in the future. The opportunity structures in her case made work in industry (supposedly) available to any Indigenous person, yet the particularities of those legal regulations were amorphous and posed some confusion on both our parts. Their ambiguity didn't push us away or move Ruth's aspirations to a different set of economic activities. Instead, that uncertainty held her at arm's length until it was convenient to employ her.

WASTE, WEALTH, AND COPPER WIRE

The differences in Destiny's and Ruth's resource-inflected aspirations are grounded in their different ties to place and divergent citizenship categories. Social class also proved to be an important dimension to the ways in which mining figured into people's aspirations for the future, even if indirectly. Bonnie is a Métis woman from a small neighbouring community. She relocated to Hay River to try to find better paying work and, by her account, "better looking men." She lived in the High Rise in the 1990s when she first arrived, but quickly met the man who would become her husband. She now lives in a middle-class home and is the mother of three grown children. I was Bonnie's daughter's third-grade teacher, so we have known each other for nearly fifteen years. Paying close attention to Bonnie's daily life, I began to see how imagining stable livelihoods despite a record of impermanence depends on integrating and reframing past failures with present aspirations for "the good life." Her story reinforces the point raised by Destiny's story: people orient to the long process of extraction more so than any single project. Likewise, Bonnie's experiences showcase some of the tensions around Indigenousness alluded to in Ruth's story. Her particular forms of aspiring attest to what Cattelino (2010) calls the "double bind of Indigenous sovereignty." While Métis women like Bonnie work hard to achieve and maintain a middle-class life, they must also simultaneously mitigate accusations that their wealth has something to do with their status as Indigenous and is therefore undeserved. As Bonnie's story will show, her resource future is much more circuitous than Destiny's; however, it is equally tense.

In June 2014, I was in Hay River doing follow-up research and was invited to meet a group of women in the industrial part of town for a volunteer project. Heaps of fuel barrels, large equipment long out of service, and oversized steel frame workshops line the side of the highway that links Hay River to southern Canada. On this summer evening, the chain link gates to a commercial electrician's yard had been left open to let in the handful of cars and SUVs that showed up within the agreed upon hour of seven o'clock. The sun at that time of year sets around midnight, giving volunteers lots of time to work. Bonnie had organized the event. A mother of three in her early forties, Bonnie is known in town as the absolute best fundraiser and volunteer coordinator. Mention her name and the reflex response is, "She gets shit done!" Tonight's task was to strip and sort heaps of copper wire discarded by one of the three diamond mines. Copper is 100 per cent recyclable and therefore one of the most valuable metals on the scrap market. The tedious task of removing any casing from around the copper increases the sale price substantially. When I arrived, Bonnie and her best friend, Joanne, were in the yard trying to estimate how much money the copper would fetch. "Thousands!" they concluded. The proceeds of the sale would all go to a community skateboard park already in progress. Both Bonnie and Joanne were mothers of boys who were aging out of their skateboard phase, so the women's commitment to the project wasn't about simply providing for their own.

That evening, armed with bulky work gloves, X-Acto knives, a new country playlist, and canned wine coolers, we stood over wooden worktables, slitting wire lengthwise in the same way we might gut fish from Great Slave Lake later that weekend. Bonnie has been a friend for a long time, so I felt comfortable expressing my frustrations to her bluntly. "How can a town in a region that continually boasts incredible economic gains from mining not have money for basic recreation and housing infrastructure? Why isn't there a revenue system in place that would save you all the trouble of non-stop fundraising?" Bonnie swatted small black flies away from her face, "That's not their job. We don't want something for nothing," she said.

This was an important moment for me. Since 2007, I had been studying the introduction and implementation of corporate ethics measures that enabled harvesting diamonds on Indigenous territory. Like others before me, it was clear that corporate forms of care came with substantial limits: they overlooked the imbalance of power between negotiating parties (Caine and Krogman 2010), they narrowly self-defined what domains would be governed (T. Li 2010), and they made use of loose protocols with "soft" legal standing (Irlbacher-Fox 2010). As I chatted with local women, I realized that corporate ethics structures, limited as they may be, offered new kinds of ethical affordances to local middle-class Métis women like Bonnie, Joanne, and the others who came to help with the copper wire that night.

Ethics is part of the human condition. Webb Keane (2015, 4) uses the term "ethical life" to refer to "those aspects of people's actions, as well as their sense of themselves and of other people, that are oriented with reference to values and ends that are not in turn defined as the means to some further ends." Against the backdrop of a growing market for "ethical gems," of which Canada is a key producer, diamond mining makes locally specific ethical affordances to Northern people.[1] Up to that point, I had been intent on thinking about how people evaluated corporations. However, in everyday interactions, it had scarcely come up. Such evaluations were relegated to formal "community consultations" (industry or activist) and generally involved a limited number of people. What was more significant, and reoccurring, was that people in the diamond basin evaluated themselves and others vis-à-vis industry. This generated a new set of questions. What is a proper relationship to industry? What does an ethical relationship to mining look like in ordinary, everyday terms in northern North America?

Bonnie's emphasis on "not getting something for nothing" made clear that she did not want to be perceived as a direct benefactor of industry. The work the women undertook to prepare the wire for sale negated it as a gift. "This would have just gone to a landfill!" was a common refrain that evening. This repositioned the women as doing the ethical work of transforming potential waste into communal wealth. Joanne kept detailed records of the number of hours people contributed to the copper wire project. She determined that people's time could be valued at C$15 per hour. Once the skate park was built, any person who volunteered would have their names alongside businesses that made cash donations.

To understand the desire to not be "getting something for nothing" and to have one's contribution to infrastructure on public display, I have to return to the broader context of the Canadian multicultural ethos and its relationship to extraction. What makes Canadian stones distinctive from others, in addition to meeting state environmental standards, is what in industry parlance is called the "social licence to operate." The "social licence to operate" in the NWT is achieved in part through provision of training and work as discussed in the last chapter, as well as contributions to large, highly visible infrastructure projects and direct one-time cash payouts to the nearest communities. These kinds of donations are typically frontloaded in a project's development. They are aimed at securing and maintaining local support. It is important to know that subarctic diamonds are not readily seen, felt, or experienced directly by most Northerners. Instead, diamonds

---

1   Ethical affordances are the opportunities that any experiences might offer as people evaluate themselves, other persons, and their circumstances (Keane 2015).

interact with everyday life through these tangible outcomes of corporate social responsibility (CSR) practices. Preferential hiring quotas and state-industry subsidized job training programs mean that almost everyone knows someone with a coveted high-wage job in the mines. Public spaces are branded with diamonds and transnational mining corporation logos. There are new hockey arenas, a homeless shelter in the region's capital city, and a new museum exhibit that rewrote the region's history to begin with diamond formation. For select Indigenous governments who received nominal one-time cash payouts in exchange for access to land, there are a small handful of new, much-needed, housing units in their communities and sometimes new trucks.

The issue with the presence of public "wealth" and corporate gifting is that it runs counter to the logic of "need-based" sovereignty. In Anglophone North America, need-based sovereignty is a key modality of settler colonialism that is premised on rights having been granted as forms of state care or aid, such as exchanging land for "help" with health issues (e.g., epidemics brought in by colonialism) and assistance with preserving lifeways (e.g., materials to facilitate hunting and trapping to avoid starvation). State forms of care and benevolence have underwritten colonial interventions since the beginning of colonization and continue through to the present (Stevenson 2014). This history means that traces of wealth in Northern communities upset settler expectations of Indigenous dependence on the state. New house constructions and large pickup trucks are read by settler society as evidence that Indigenous people no longer need "special rights." Northern Indigenous groups confront a double bind best described by Jessica Cattelino (2010). This double bind works as follows: Indigenous sovereigns, such as American Indian tribal nations and Canadian First Nations, require economic resources to exercise sovereignty, and their revenues often derive from their governmental rights; however, once they exercise economic power, the legitimacy of Indigenous sovereignty and citizenship is challenged within settler society. This is precisely the case in the NWT, where 50 per cent of the population that is non-Indigenous largely believes that much of local wealth has not been "earned"; rather, it has simply been given. Or, put differently, now that there is a visible Indigenous middle class in the territory's few urban centres, such "benefits" to this set of citizens should cease.

Tensions over Indigenous rights are always just below the surface of many conversations in the town where I have worked for ten years. Sometimes, they erupt. Bonnie often found herself in confrontations with her settler "frenemy," Lacy. At the local pub, Lacy would often launch into attacks that Bonnie should no longer be getting "free stuff from the government." Bonnie comes from one of the most famous fur-trapping families in the region. Part of her rights as a Métis are subsidized equipment for hunting and trapping, which are activities her family does regularly. Bonnie, a self-described "bad-ass Métis woman," had no trouble defending her rights to Lacy and reminding her she was in fact a guest on this territory. While Bonnie could shake off these outwardly racist confrontations, I began to see how much of her work as a community volunteer was aimed at countering these dominant cultural narratives. For Joanne to count people's hours to convert them to public accounts of "work" all of sudden made a new kind of sense to me. The marketing of ethical diamonds as doing "more for communities" sets into motion practices that make industry's benevolent presence felt and seen. This doesn't only subject industry to evaluation, but it also encourages the evaluation of those people/groups who are understood to be on the receiving end of social policy. In everyday life, middle-class Indigenous people have to hold at bay potential evaluations of their un-deservingness. Volunteerism interrupts potential evaluations of being non-contributing members of the community.

During the 2008–9 financial crisis, large donations from corporations to communities were in significant decline. Global trends in CSR began to stress that too many gifts would create unsustainable dependence on industry. As one CSR consultant-anthropologist put it at a national mining conference I attended, "It is not charity that we do, it's mining." In northern Canada, fundraising events like selling copper, organizing raffle draws, and hosting bingo nights helped to compensate for the state's decreasing provision of social service programs and an increased dependence on direct precarious Industry-community partnerships. When contributions were in decline, critical evaluations of industry were scarce, in part because of the prevalence of volunteerism that emerged at the intersection of visible industry gifts and long-standing racial inequalities. As Andrea Muehlebach (2012) argues in her book, *The Moral Neoliberal*, morality is an indispensable tool for capitalist transformation. Northern fundraising events are not only a means of dealing with the economic realities of late industrialism in the subarctic; they are also critical sites of ethical cultivation and self-fashioning among the subarctic's small but growing Indigenous middle class. Specifically, women's work to convert mine waste (copper wire) into longer lasting wealth (children's recreation facilities) was repeatedly held up as evidence that they were not "getting something for nothing" from the mines. Local ethical frameworks have long prioritized collective accumulation and redistribution of local wealth; however, in the shadow of large-scale resource development, it takes on new narrative forms.

CONCLUSION

In her book *Still Life: Hopes, Desires and Satisfactions,* British anthropologist Henrietta Moore (2011, 23) describes culture as the "art of living," which includes how people think about the future. Hoping, desiring, and aspiring all share the "forward direction of our appetite for attachment to the world, to ourselves, to objects, to others and to the relationships we establish between all these things and the meanings and value we create and attribute to them." Conjuring a future helps to create the tracks along which action is pushed (Weber 1948). In this way, aspiration is a critical component of northern Canada's extractive present and future.

While extractive industry created peri-urbanization and an expanded middle class, middle-class aspirations and actions aren't so straightforward for everyone, as we see with Bonnie and Joanne. Liberal forms of multicultural recognition mean that middle-classness undermines forms of ethnic citizenship. As a result, middle-class Indigenous women have developed intricate strategies (like volunteerism) for creating arm's length ways of making resource futures for themselves and their families. Anthropologists have argued that the middle class is a critical site for considering the implications of globalization (Heiman, Freeman, and Leichty 2012). The emergence of a middle class in places like Alaska, Greenland, Finland, and the Canadian Arctic is rarely taken up in social scientific research as a topic; more still, there is seldom even an acknowledgment of class differentiation at all (except Dombrowksi 2001). The focus instead is on homogenous cultural groups under siege by capitalism and globalization. This misses the opportunity to track the full diversity of lifeways that constitute Northern communities, all of which make global extraction possible and profitable.

For all the women I have described here, resource-entangled futures were differentiated by race, class, and citizenship. What is worth noticing is how they create forms of aspiring that are reliant on mining without being explicitly so. This arm's-length aspiration is a key element in the architecture of extraction. It holds the possibility of disappointment without blame. As nobody depends on any one project, a single failure does not produce charged political sentiments. Equally, it holds the possibility of success without giving industry credit. In this way, middle-class people, like me, might imagine that their hard work in chasing their aspirations is what led to their current successes.

DISCUSSION QUESTIONS

1 How would you describe the meaning of affect? Is it a concept that resonates with you? Can you think of examples where the term "affect" would help you explain an event or experience?
2 Think about some of the aspirations you have for your future. What are the "opportunity structures" that are shaping those desires?
3 Thinking about this chapter, describe an example of the relationship between corporate ethics and ordinary ethics?
4 The author argues that being middle class isn't straightforward for Indigenous women. Why is that the case?

CHAPTER EIGHT

Conclusion

DIAMONDS DO GOOD?

In June 2018, the Government of the Northwest Territories was awarded a "Diamonds Do Good Award" from the Diamond Empowerment Fund, a global non-profit organization that self-describes as being "inspired by Nelson Mandela and founded by leaders in the diamond industry to empower diamond communities around the world" (Government of Northwest Territories 2018a). The award was meant to recognize the government's responsible, sustainable management of the NWT's diamond industry. The announcement of the award was the opening story for the 2018 summary of the socio-economic impact assessment for the diamond industry. Instead of being a neutral-sounding assessment of the industry, the glossy, colourful pages and upbeat rhetoric made the brochure indistinguishable from corporations' own accounts of their businesses.

In accepting the award, the premier of the NWT remarked, "In short, diamond mining has allowed the people of the Northwest Territories to take control of their future" (Government of Northwest Territories 2018b). This statement held my attention for some time. In a region where Indigenous rights and self-determination are ongoing battles, what does it mean for a political leader to emphasize "control" over the future? Expedited mineral development in the NWT, much like extractive industry across the circumpolar world

(Alaska, Finland), is promoted as granting Indigenous people and Arctic residents the fiscal means to enact autonomy and build futures in their image. To some extent, this is not wholly untrue. Revenue generated from extraction is harnessed by communities and governments to create architectures of a good life for now and for future generations. This includes physical infrastructure like better roads and water service, and political-legal structures like land claim and self-government agreements. Recent research on mining and Indigeneity has been quick to point out that Indigenous peoples aren't simply industry's victims. Resource activity can be harnessed to Indigenous aims (Sawyer and Gomez 2012; Slowey 2008). At the same time, there is an affective shift that naturalizes this type of large-scale development as the best, easiest, and perhaps an inevitable form of economic growth and prioritizes market-based solutions to social inequality (Cameron and Levitan 2014).

The premier's optimism needs to be balanced with the stories of the men and women I shared in this book. These are people whose futures are indeed entangled with diamond mining and extraction more broadly, albeit not in uniform ways. The back and forth between the ways in which people in the NWT enact agency over their futures and the ways in which the whims of industry exert a force on their pathways makes the notion of "control" seem decidedly oversimplified.

Over the course of the book, I shared the stories of Ruth, Destiny, and Trevor as they enrolled in an underground mine training course. I showed how their paths unfolded differently in the context of different ethnic, gendered, and class backgrounds, as well as in the context of the global financial crisis. The summer before their course began (2008), there was a lot of optimism for underground mining. The Snap Lake mine, owned by De Beers, was the third diamond mine to open in the region. Unlike its two predecessors, it was fully underground. Soon after, in 2009, all the mines froze all hiring as the global financial crisis began to affect the industry. Though hiring eventually resumed, by December 2015, De Beers announced it was closing the underground mine and laid off 434 workers. The closure came in the wake of a downturn in diamond prices alongside water problems at the mine that required an expensive amendment to the mine's water licence. On the heels of this closure, De Beers, along with their partner, Mountain Province, opened the NWT's fourth mine, Gahcho Kué, in

2016. These overlapping openings and closings have meant that for many residents of the NWT, there is a permanence to the process of extraction, even if single projects come and go. The particular temporality of mining in the NWT is a critical element in the affective architecture of extraction.

At the "Diamonds Do Good" awards gala, two NWT residents, both Métis women and employees of the Gahcho Kué and Diavik mines, joined the premier. The women were lauded in the report for being "independent" and "hav[ing] embraced the opportunities provided by responsible diamond mining to establish and grow their careers in the NWT's world-class diamond sector" (Government of Northwest Territories 2018b). This framing does the work of enshrining the industry as a moral actor and puts forward the notion that Indigenous women can, and should, become beacons of responsible futuremaking through individual wage work in the primary sector. The stories of Ruth, Destiny, and Bonnie make clear how different kinds of women are not always able to, or interested in, enacting resource futures in the ways that the state and corporations imagine.

For the last twenty years, I have lived and worked on and off in different parts of the circumpolar world that are in close proximity to large-scale mining projects (diamonds in Canada, copper and gold in Alaska, iron ore in Finland). At the same time, these are places where evidence of differentially distributed social harm is apparent to everyone. Northern rural Indigenous populations have, on average, lower life expectancies and live on lower household incomes than their non-Indigenous (white) southern counterparts. Given my background, I am often asked: "Is mining good or bad for Indigenous people?" Mining's possible "goodness" generally indexes imagined jobs and business contract opportunities. Natural resource development's "badness" stems from concerns about loss of "tradition," destruction of the environment, and the dislocation of existing social relations. Mining, and the industrialization of the circumpolar world more generally, is often portrayed as either straightforward losses of local traditions and culture or as gains couched in terms of modernization and development. When the first two industrial diamond mines opened in the early 2000s, natural resources in general, and diamonds in particular, were discussed as either a cure to diminish Indigenous poverty or as a curse that would extend the history of colonialism and exploitation. What the curse-versus-cure debates overlook are the intricate ways in which the people most directly affected by mining projects, both Indigenous and not, orient to the promises, fulfilled and not, of resource development and how, in turn, these promises shape what kinds of imagined futures are possible. What I hope my fieldwork in an urbanizing community in the Northwest Territories has shown is that the curse-or-cure dichotomy obscures the myriad ways that local, national, and international subjects have worked within and against the currents of industrial development over the last century.

This book is not intended as a counterpoint to the notion that "diamonds do good." My point isn't that "diamonds do bad." Diamonds aren't agents acting alone. Instead, they are a single commodity in a historic stream of resources that have been harvested in northern Canada for consumption in other parts of the world. Mapping the social, political, and environmental harms that come from swift resource development was a cornerstone in the emergence of an anthropology of mining in the 1970s, when mineral activity spiked globally (Ballard and Banks 2003). Because of this intellectual history, in effort to mount political critiques of industry, activists and academics alike researching Arctic extraction continue to take a single resource project as a target of scrutiny and focus on questions of negative impacts. Perhaps because of state and industry optimism, criticisms are usually heavy handed and emphasize local forms of resistance to extraction in general, and to colonialism more particularly (Hall 2017, 2022). While these are valuable interventions, the on-the-ground realities of ordinary men and women, Indigenous and not, can be lost to political theorizing. In conceptualizing an approach that emphasizes the architecture of extraction, my aim is to offer a way to understand Arctic extraction from the vantage point of the people it affects, often in very subtle ways. In the face of mine development and the "grey zones" of Indigenous politics and life (Starn 2011), Stuart Kirsch (2007, 303) suggests, "anthropologists need ethnographic accounts that analyze the complex ambitions of [I]ndigenous movements." Writing in reference to strategies of counter-globalization deployed by Indigenous social movements in Papua New Guinea, Kirsch was drawn into "politics" that was recognizable as such (protests, actions, claims being advanced). I have been interested here in "the political" that isn't easily straightforwardly apprehended – that is, those emergent forms of political living that dwell in the interstices of extraction and Indigeneity, as well as those beyond it.

The particular qualities of the diamond have provided an apposite metaphor for the approach I have taken in this book. As light travels through a diamond, it is dispersed. As a reminder, dispersion is the term for the breaking up of white light into its spectral colours so that they are individually visible to the human eye. A diamond doesn't produce rainbows; it simply allows us to see them. In the same way, in the Northwest Territories, mining alone doesn't produce poor housing, high food costs, diabetes, or domestic violence as it is often assumed in popular media. What mining does, through public culture, politics, and practice, is make visible the contradictions of economic and governmental forms (specifically, extractive industry and multicultural recognition). While contrasts of resource wealth and racialized poverty enable us to see disparity, they also foreclose other ways of approaching the issues at hand and understanding the ways diverse Northern people do craft "good lives" amid instability. Through the prism of diamonds, a much wider set of necessary relationships that sustain extraction come into view. By relying on the notion of "architecture," we get a wider view, historically and ethnographically, of the ways in which the Arctic has become a key global site for resource extraction. While the state and industry (and some social scientists) continue to evaluate mining projects one at a time, my choice to move away from the singular focus on diamonds to the broader analysis of architectures of extraction is my way of overcoming corporate social responsibility's reliance on, and reproduction of, a highly chronotopically constrained way of understanding culture and economy.

Since the late 1940s, thanks to the famed De Beers advertising campaign, diamonds are the North American icon for "forever." Even with the reality that half of North American marriages will end in divorce, a diamond engagement ring's power to signify an eternity together has not faded. Diamond mining does not come with the same promise. Much the opposite. A mine's closure is a given. Resources run out. Under the banner of corporate transparency, mines often make public their planned closure date and plan. The mine's "lifecycle" may be exaggerated in that plan as these plans don't forecast changing markets and economic conditions that lead to early closure or production freezes. Even still, amid such uncertainty, it is still possible for local people to try to exert some control over their futures and imagine that mining just might make them "set for life."

THE FIRE

I received a photo of billows of black smoke coming from the High Rise via text in March 2019. As the day went on, the same photo and the accompanying news story were sent to me multiple times from various friends living in the NWT. The High Rise had a massive fire. All 150 tenants were evacuated, and temporary shelters were set up in the town's recreation centre, in the friendship centre, and on the K'atl'odeeche First Nation reserve. The cause of the fire was unknown. To this day, there is nothing conclusive about how, or perhaps who, started the blaze. As I write in 2022, the High Rise remains condemned. Residents have not been allowed to move back in. Many found other sources of housing, while some people continue to be without permanent shelter. The local newspaper estimates that over a dozen people, primarily Indigenous residents, including some elderly people, have yet to find stable housing.

One news story (Desmarais 2020) tells of Racheal, a middle-aged Indigenous woman who spent years being denied an apartment in the High Rise because of her criminal record. Not long after she finally secured a unit, the fire happened. The day that tenants were allowed back into the building to get their belongings, Racheal filled a shopping cart with her most precious belongings, photos of her late daughter and Montreal Canadiens paraphernalia. A year after the fire, her housing situation remains uncertain. What the news accounts reveal is that those who have already experienced the most hardship suffer the consequences of these kinds of events more deeply than others.

The local media buzzed about the issue for some time after the fire. Each article offered different analyses of the situation but primarily settled on one of two explanations. First, many commentators pointed the finger at the building's owner, who left town not long after the fire and has seldom returned. There was no fire insurance on the building (something legal in this part of Canada but unheard of elsewhere). The costs of repair would need to come from the property management company, which is nearly bankrupt, from what I understand.

This line of thinking posits that the bad acts of one individual explain this outcome. Second, some politicians and residents think that the fire shows just how bad the Northern housing shortage is. What is not asked in this scenario is under what conditions are housing shortages created and maintained? It is not simply a matter of the absence of the appropriate number of dwellings. On many of my walks around town, I noticed empty units. Windows with their curtains drawn back revealed empty houses. Some of these houses were held by a private realtor who preferred to rent to high-paying corporate clients versus local people. Others were part of the territorial social housing stock but had fallen into disrepair. Much like the High Rise, the state of these units is often blamed on the tenants. Akin to the situation in northern Australia described by Lea and Pholeros (2010, 187), Indigenous householders and their behaviours are understood by media and policy makers as culprits for the state of disrepair rather than the "substandard original construction, under-supervised repairs, poor to nonexistent maintenance, and rapid shifts in policy attention" (see also Christensen 2017). My hope is that at this point in the book, the notion of architecture of extraction would help to convince you that individualistic explanations (whether about tenants or the owner) could not possibly suffice. Even something larger like a housing shortage cannot be separated from the North's resource-based economy. Events like the fire, upon some reflection, reveal how mining generates spaces of hope for many while simultaneously producing vulnerabilities for others.

None of the people I introduced in this book still lived in the High Rise by the time of the fire. Cindy, Trevor's mom, broke things off with the owner a few years earlier. She moved to Saskatchewan to be closer to Trevor and to help with care for his twins and the two other children he has had in the interim years. The people I introduced in chapter 5 (Chris, Ivan, Billy, Gary, Marion) were no longer tenants when I returned for follow-up fieldwork in 2014. I am not sure where their paths led them. Destiny has been back and forth to Hay River from Edmonton but never long enough to say she lives there. Her story in recent years is not mine to tell. We keep in touch, and I know the broad outlines of her movements, hopes, and plans, but I feel as though the specifics are now the property of our friendship and not my research. I will say that she decided to enrol her daughter with

Figure 8.1. Mackenzie Place in early spring.
Source: Photo by Jesse Colin Jackson 2013.

her now ex-partner's band. This has caused some stress, as accessing social services requires her daughter to be in the area. In some ways, this forecloses the possibility that Destiny will return to Hay River, as more options for housing and other supports are tied to the area south of Hay River or are more readily available in Edmonton, the closest urban centre. You might say these factors pushed her out of the NWT, but she wouldn't see it that way. She is strident that she is the maker of her own path and – as her chosen pseudonym indicates – her destiny.

After the fire, the High Rise was purchased by what a local newspaper described as "a sophisticated Western Canadian company" (Whitehouse 2022a). The company, Heritage Valley Capital, has a limited web presence. They self-describe as "providing double digit returns for investors looking for passive, secure income … through real estate development projects and cash flow products" (Heritage Valley Capital, n.d.). The purchase of the High Rise is the latest iteration what I called infrastructural prospecting in chapter 4. Past failures become future extractive opportunities for those who can afford them. Some local politicians estimate an influx of in-migrants when a nearby lead/zinc mine opens and a fish plant renovates. These prospective resource projects enliven ideas that new ways to prosper are right around the corner.

In talking to local media about plans to renovate the High Rise, the investors imagine the desires and aspirations of future tenants who are not yet there. One developer commented, "There's nothing stopping that building from having a gym, having a theatre, having a quartz countertop and being the same that you would get in Toronto, Montreal, Vancouver, Surrey or wherever" (Whitehouse 2022b). The statement echoes the earliest advertisements for the High Rise, promising modern amenities on par with cities like Calgary. The company projects particular forms of aspiration onto the future of this Northern community as if these were value-neutral, natural, universal wants (quartz counters). These imagined future tenants drive the vision for the renovation (and not someone like Racheal). The investors' ideas reflect some, but not all, local desires and visions for the future. They certainly do not capture the complexity of housing needs and wants in the community. The investors told local news that their aim was to help address the region's housing shortage, but just who will be housed in the next iteration of the High Rise is unclear. As of August

2022, no work has been done on the property. Events like the High Rise fire, upon some reflection, reveal how mining generates spaces of hope for many while simultaneously excaerbating vulnerabilities.

The High Rise is the outcome of an architecture of extraction that enabled rapid forms of industrial development and prioritized the needs and wants of companies and local elites over the general population. Much of the trajectory of the town of Hay River can be understood in the same way. The paved roads, the barge system, and the railway are all physical infrastructure from previous resource booms that serve the present. These changes also enable an influx of people to work in these industries, like the ones I described in chapter 5. However, because of the erratic nature of natural resource work, the population is unstable, and therefore so are the rents collected in the High Rise. The upkeep of a building intended for a southern city was difficult from the day the building opened its doors, as I learned from Albert, the building's first manager (chapter 4). The arrival of more settlers had other effects as well. It heightened and intensified racial tensions and inequality, leading to a new era of legislation aimed at trying to remedy the situation and secure Indigenous rights (like the formation of the reservation described in chapter 3). Other changes were less tangible but no less significant, like the rise of a middle class and their accordant aspirations driving the economy to reflect their desires and visions for the future. Northern Canada's architecture of extraction is complex and involves the elements I have described in this book, yet it is also always emergent. This means that the diamond story is in the process of being written and rewritten and can't be neatly concluded here.

My hope is that the lens of architecture of extraction has "made strange" the viewing of inequality through the prism of diamonds (or any resource for that matter). Of course, many Northern people experience social harm that can (and should) be traced to an extractive economy. That said, people often experience suffering in rather ordinary and routine ways, as these elements have structured the better part of their life trajectories. My objective in the book was not simply to describe the experiences of everyday difficulties, but rather to try to explain how everyday obstacles and distress articulate within and against larger forms of difference and inequality in order to show how relations of inequality are reproduced in part through the routinization of violence (Das 2007). What's more, as we saw in chapters 2 and 6, notions of Indigenous social suffering make the creation of "ethical diamonds" possible. Somewhat counterintuitively, an overemphasis on the negative aspects of industry seems to shore up more support for it. The tools of anthropology are well suited to documenting these contradictions and complexities rather than sweeping them under the rug. Natural resource extraction undoubtedly puts pressure on Northern people, both individually and collectively. At the same time, Northern and Indigenous people put pressure on industry. I would argue that the everyday experience of these pressures is what animates the shape of northern resource development more so than any one specific policy or legislation.

Our lives are filled with objects that came from other parts of the world. Many of us, myself included, want to consider how to move processes of production and consumption towards more ethical and equitable outcomes for people and environments. That isn't always easy to do. We may get overwhelmed and feel that there is no use in individual consumer–driven equality schemes. My hope is not that we don't throw in the ethical towel but rather that we get curious about our framing of the problems themselves. I offer architecture of extraction as a way of broadening the types of questions one asks when faced with the moral dilemma of being a person in a consumer society. It is a way to understand the intersection of global and local forces by centring the everyday.

DISCUSSION QUESTIONS

1 Is there a way to describe the relationship between mining and inequality?
2 How do you understand the term "architecture of extraction"?
3 Identify a product that is marketed for its ethical values. How would you think anthropologically about the product's claims? What questions would you ask to gain a deeper understanding of the issues at play?

References

Agha, Asif. 2004. "Registers of Language." In *A Companion to Linguistic Anthropology*, edited by Alessandro Duranti, 23–45. Oxford: Blackwell. https://doi.org/10.1002/9780470996522.ch2.

———. 2005. "Voice, Footing, Enregisterment." *Journal of Linguistic Anthropology* 15, no. 1 (May): 38–59. https://doi.org/10.1525/jlin.2005.15.1.38.

———. 2011. "Commodity Registers." *Journal of Linguistic Anthropology* 21, no. 1 (June): 22–53. https://doi.org/10.1111/j.1548-1395.2011.01081.x.

Allan, Kori L. 2014. "Learning How to 'Skill' the Self: Citizenship and Immigrant Integration in Toronto, Canada." Unpublished PhD diss., University of Toronto.

Amadena Investments. 2017. "Foxfire Diamond." Cision PR Newswire, March 19, 2017. https://www.prnewswire.com/news-releases/amadena-investments-announces-foxfire-diamond-exhibit-extended-at-the-smithsonian-300420898.html.

Anand, Nikhil. 2011. "PRESSURE: The PoliTechnics of Water Supply in Mumbai." *Cultural Anthropology* 26, no. 4 (November): 542–64. https://doi.org/10.1111/j.1548-1360.2011.01111.x.

Anand, Nikhil, Akhil Gupta, and Hannah Appel, eds. 2018. *The Promise of Infrastructure*. Durham: Duke University Press. https://doi.org/10.2307/j.ctv12101q3.

Arsel, Murat, Barbara Hogenboom, and Lorenzo Pellegrini. 2016. "The Extractive Imperative in Latin America." *The Extractive Industries and Society* 3, no. 4 (November): 880–7. https://doi.org/10.1016/j.exis.2016.10.014.

Asad, Talal. 1979. "Anthropology and the Analysis of Ideology." *Man* 14, no. 4 (December): 607–27. https://doi.org/10.2307/2802150.

Asch, Michael. 1977. "The Dene Economy." In Watkins 1977, 47–61. https://doi.org/10.3138/9781487574451-010.

———. 1979. "The Ecological-Evolutionary Model and the Concept of Mode of Production: Two Approaches to Material Reproduction." In *Challenging Anthropology: A Critical Introduction to Social and Cultural Anthropology*, edited by David M. Turner and Gavin A. Smith, 81–99. Toronto: McGraw-Hill Ryerson.

Bakhtin, Mikhail Mikhaîlovich. 1981. *The Dialogic Imagination: Four Essays.* Edited by Michael Holquist. Translated by Michael Holquist and Caryl Emerson. Austin: University of Texas Press.

Ballard, Chris, and Glenn Banks. 2003. "Resource Wars: The Anthropology of Mining." *Annual Review of Anthropology* 32: 287–313. https://doi.org/10.1146/annurev.anthro.32.061002.093116.

Barnett, Clive, Paul Cloke, Nick Clarke, and Alice Malpass. 2011. *Globalizing Responsibility: The Political Rationalities of Ethical Consumption.* Oxford: Wiley-Blackwell. https://doi.org/10.1002/9781444390216.

Bell, Lindsay A. 2012. "In Search of Hope: Mobility and Citizenships on the Canadian Frontier." In *Migration in the 21st Century: Political Economy and Ethnography*, edited by Pauline Gardiner Barber and Winnie Lem, 132–52. New York: Routledge. https://doi.org/10.4324/9780203116494.

———. 2017. "Soft Skills, Hard Rocks: Making Diamonds Ethical in Canada's Northwest Territories." *Focaal* 2017, no. 79 (June): 74–88. https://doi.org/10.3167/fcl.2017.790107.

Berlan, Amanda. 2012. "Making or Marketing a Difference? An Anthropological Examination of the Marketing of Fair Trade Cocoa From Ghana." In *Hidden Hands in the Market: Ethnographies of Fair Trade, Ethical Consumption, and Corporate Social Responsibility*, edited by Geert de Neve, Peter Luetchford, Jeffrey Pratt, and Donald C. Wood, 171–94. Bingley: Emerald Group Publishing. https://doi.org/10.1016/S0190-1281(08)28008-X.

Besky, Sarah. 2013. *The Darjeeling Distinction: Labor and Justice on Fair-Trade Tea Plantations in India.* 1st ed. Berkeley: University of California Press. https://doi.org/10.1525/9780520957602.

Bielawski, Ellen. 2004. *Rogue Diamonds.* Seattle: University of Washington Press.

Brilliant Earth. n.d.-a. "Brilliant Earth – Sustainable Bridal & Fine Jewelry." Accessed November 30, 2022. https://www.brilliantearth.com/.

———. n.d.-b. "Canadian Diamonds." Accessed November 30, 2022. https://www.brilliantearth.com/diamond/canadian/.

Brown, Jennifer. 1993. "Fur Trade History as Text and Drama." In *The Uncovered Past: Roots of Northern Alberta Societies*, edited by Patricia A. McCormack and R. Geoffrey Ironside, 81–8. Circumpolar Research Series 3. Edmonton: Canadian Circumpolar Institute, University of Alberta.

Burley, Edith. 1997. *Servants of the Honourable Company: Work, Discipline, and Conflict in the Hudson's Bay Company, 1770–1870.* Canadian Social History Series. Toronto: Oxford University Press.

Byers, Michael. 2009. *Who Owns the Arctic? Understanding Sovereignty Disputes in the North*. Vancouver: Douglas & McIntyre.

Caine, Ken J., and Naomi Krogman. 2010. "Powerful or Just Plain Power-Full? A Power Analysis of Impact and Benefit Agreements in Canada's North." *Organization & Environment* 23, no. 1 (March): 76–98. https://doi.org/10.1177/1086026609358969.

Cameron, Deborah. 2000. "Styling the Worker: Gender and the Commodification of Language in the Globalized Service Economy." *Journal of Sociolinguistics* 4, no. 3 (August): 323–47. https://doi.org/10.1111/1467-9481.00119.

Cameron, Emilie, and Tyler Levitan. 2014. "Impact and Benefit Agreements and the Neoliberalization of Resource Governance and Indigenous-State Relations in Northern Canada." *Studies in Political Economy* 93, no. 1 (March): 25–52. https://doi.org/10.1080/19187033.2014.11674963.

Campbell, Karen. 2004. *Undermining Our Future: How Mining's Privileged Access to Land Harms People and the Environment – A Discussion Paper on the Need to Reform Mineral Tenure Law in Canada*. Vancouver: West Coast Environmental Law. https://www.wcel.org/publication/undermining-our-future-how-minings-privileged-access-land-harms-people-and-environment.

Canada Diamonds. n.d. "Wholesale Canadian Diamonds, Engagement Rings, GIA and AGS Ideal Cut Certified Diamonds, Wedding Bands, Platinum Jewellery Direct from Diamond Broker." Accessed November 30, 2022. https://www.canadadiamonds.com/.

Canadian Diamond Code of Conduct. 2002. "The Canadian Diamond Code of Conduct – The Code." Accessed February 15, 2008. https://www.canadiandiamondcodeofconduct.ca/EN_code.htm.

Carr, E. Summerson. 2010. *Scripting Addiction: The Politics of Therapeutic Talk and American Sobriety*. Princeton: Princeton University Press. https://doi.org/10.1515/9781400836659.

Carrier, James G. 2010. "Protecting the Environment the Natural Way: Ethical Consumption and Commodity Fetishism." *Antipode* 42, no. 3 (June): 672–89. https://doi.org/10.1111/j.1467-8330.2010.00768.x.

———. 2018. "Moral Economy: What's in a Name." *Anthropological Theory* 18, no. 1 (March): 18–35. https://doi.org/10.1177/1463499617735259.

Cater, Tara. 2017. "Making Fly-In-Fly-Out (FIFO) Work: Multiple Temporalities and Social Reproduction in Rankin Inlet, Nunavut." *Society and Space*, November 14, 2017. https://www.societyandspace.org/articles/making-fly-in-fly-out-fifo-work-multiple-temporalities-and-social-reproduction-in-rankin-inlet-nunavut.

Cattelino, Jessica R. 2010. "The Double Bind of American Indian Need-Based Sovereignty." *Cultural Anthropology* 25, no. 2 (May): 235–62. https://doi.org/10.1111/j.1548-1360.2010.01058.x.

Cavanaugh, Jillian R., and Shalini Shankar. 2012. "Language and Materiality in Global Capitalism." *Annual Review of Anthropology* 41: 335–69. https://doi.org/10.1146/annurev-anthro-092611-145811.

———. 2014. "Producing Authenticity in Global Capitalism: Language, Materiality, and Value." *American Anthropologist* 116, no. 1 (March): 51–64. https://doi.org/10.1111/aman.12075.

Cazden, Courtney. 1974. "Play and Metalinguistic Awareness: One Dimension of Language Experience." *The Urban Review* 7, no. 1 (January): 28–39. https://doi.org/10.1007/BF02223202.

CBC. 2009. "Northern Roadside Attractions Grace Canada Post Stamps." *CBC News*, July 7, 2009, sec. North. https://www.cbc.ca/news/canada/north/northern-roadside-attractions-grace-canada-post-stamps-1.852238.

ChartHouse Learning. n.d. "Fish! the Book – FISH! Philosophy Training." Accessed November 30, 2022. https://www.fishphilosophy.com/fish-book/.

Christensen, Julia. 2016. "Indigenous Housing and Health in the Canadian North: Revisiting Cultural Safety." *Health and Place* 40 (July): 83–90. https://doi.org/10.1016/j.healthplace.2016.05.003.

———. 2017. *No Home in a Homeland: Indigenous Peoples and Homelessness in the Canadian North.* Vancouver: UBC Press.

Coates, Ken. 1993. *Best Left as Indians: Native-White Relations in the Yukon Territory, 1840–1973.* 1st edition. Montreal: McGill-Queen's University Press.

Coates, Kenneth, and William R. Morrison, eds. 1986a. *Interpreting Canada's North: Selected Readings.* New Canadian Readings. Toronto: Copp Clark Pitman.

———, eds. 1986b. *Treaty Research Report: Treaty Five 1875–1908.* Ottawa: Indian and Northern Affairs Canada.

Coloma, Roland Sintos, Bonnie McElhinny, Ethel Tungohan, John Paul Catungal, and Lisa M. Davidson, eds. 2012. *Filipinos in Canada: Disturbing Invisibility.* Toronto: University of Toronto Press. https://doi.org/10.3138/9781442662728.

Cooke, Martin, and Danièle Bélanger. 2006. "Migration Theories and First Nations Mobility: Towards a Systems Perspective." *Canadian Review of Sociology / Revue canadienne de sociologie* 43, no. 2 (May): 141–64. https://doi.org/10.1111/j.1755-618X.2006.tb02217.x.

Cooper, Frederick, and Ann Laura Stoler, eds. 1997. *Tensions of Empire: Colonial Cultures in a Bourgeois World.* Berkeley: University of California Press. https://doi.org/10.1525/9780520918085.

Coronil, Fernando. 1997. *The Magical State: Nature, Money, and Modernity in Venezuela.* Chicago: University of Chicago Press.

Coulthard, Glen Sean. 2014. *Red Skin, White Masks: Rejecting the Colonial Politics of Recognition.* Minneapolis: University of Minnesota Press. https://doi.org/10.5749/minnesota/9780816679645.001.0001.

Coulthard, Glen, and Leanne Betasamosake Simpson. 2016. "Grounded Normativity / Place-Based Solidarity." *American Quarterly* 68, no. 2 (June): 249–55. https://doi.org/10.1353/aq.2016.0038.

Coumans, Catherine. 2011. "Occupying Spaces Created by Conflict: Anthropologists, Development NGOs, Responsible Investment, and Mining." *Current Anthropology* 52, no. S3 (April): S29–43. https://doi.org/10.1086/656473.

Cremin, Colin. 2010. "Never Employable Enough: The (Im)Possibility of Satisfying the Boss's Desire." *Organization* 17, no. 2 (March): 131–49. https://doi.org/10.1177/1350508409341112.

Cummins, Emily R., and Linda M. Blum. 2015. "'Suits To Self-Sufficiency': Dress for Success and Neoliberal Maternalism." *Gender & Society* 29, no. 5 (October): 623–46. https://doi.org/10.1177/0891243215591949.

Das, Veena. 2007. *Life and Words: Violence and the Descent into the Ordinary*. Berkeley: University of California Press. https://doi.org/10.1525/9780520939530.

De Boeck, Filip. 2008. "Diamonds Without Borders: A Short History of Diamond Digging and Smuggling on the Border Between the Democratic Republic of Congo and Angola (1980–2008)." In Vlassenroot and Van Bockstael 2008, 41–55.

Deloria, Philip Joseph. 2004. *Indians in Unexpected Places*. Lawrence: University Press of Kansas.

Deloria, Vine, Jr. 1969. *Custer Died for Your Sins*. New York: Macmillan.

Desmarais, Anna. 2020. "Few Answers on Hay River Highrise Fire, 1 Year Later." *CBC News*, March 15, 2020. https://www.cbc.ca/news/canada/north/hay-river-highrise-fire-one-year-1.5497552.

Diamonds with a Story. n.d. "Diavik Sourced Diamonds." Accessed August 10, 2022. http://diamondswithastory.com/mines/diavik/.

Dokis, Carly. 2016. "Shapeshifters, the Petrostate, and the Making of Uncertain Futures in the Canadian North." *Hot Spots, Fieldsights* (blog). Society for Cultural Anthropology, July 29, 2016. https://culanth.org/fieldsights/shapeshifters-the-petrostate-and-the-making-of-uncertain-futures-in-the-canadian-north.

Dombrowski, Kirk. 2001. *Against Culture: Development, Politics, and Religion in Indian Alaska*. Lincoln: University of Nebraska Press.

———. 2008. "Reply: What's Changed (Since 1975)?" *Dialectical Anthropology* 32, nos. 1–2 (June): 43–50. https://doi.org/10.1007/s10624-008-9055-8.

———. 2010. "The White Hand of Capitalism and the End of Indigenism as We Know It." *Australian Journal of Anthropology* 21, no. 1 (April): 129–40. https://doi.org/10.1111/j.1757-6547.2010.00071.x.

Dourish, Paul, and Genevieve Bell. 2007. "The Infrastructure of Experience and the Experience of Infrastructure: Meaning and Structure in Everyday Encounters with Space." *Environment and Planning B: Planning and Design* 34, no. 3 (June): 414–30. https://doi.org/10.1068/b32035t.

DuBois, W.E.B. 1903. *The Souls of Black Folk*. Cambridge: University Press –
John Wilson and Son.

Duchêne, Alexandre, and Monica Heller, eds. 2012. *Language in Late
Capitalism: Pride and Profit*. New York: Routledge. https://doi.org
/10.4324/9780203155868.

Dybbroe, Susanne, Jens Dahl, and Ludger Müller-Wille. 2010. "Dynamics
of Arctic Urbanization." *Acta Borealia* 27, no. 2 (December): 120–4.
https://doi.org/10.1080/08003831.2010.527526.

Eagleton, Terry. 2003. *After Theory*. London: Penguin Books.

Erasmus, Georges. 1977. "We The Dene." In Watkins 1977, 177–81.
https://doi.org/10.3138/9781487574451-020.

Erlich, Edward I., and W. Dan Hausel. 2002. *Diamond Deposits: Origin,
Exploration, and History of Discovery*. Illustrated edition. Littleton: Society
for Mining, Metallurgy, and Exploration.

Fairbanks, Robert P. 2009. *How It Works: Recovering Citizens in Post-Welfare
Philadelphia*. Chicago: University of Chicago Press.

Falls, Susan. 2011. "Picturing Blood Diamonds." *Critical Arts* 25, no. 3
(September): 441–66. https://doi.org/10.1080/02560046.2011.615144.

———. 2014. *Clarity, Cut, and Culture: The Many Meanings of Diamonds*.
New York: New York University Press. https://doi.org/10.18574/nyu
/9781479810666.001.0001.

Farish, Matthew, and P. Whitney Lackenbauer. 2009. "High Modernism
in the Arctic: Planning Frobisher Bay and Inuvik." *Journal of Historical
Geography* 35, no. 3 (July): 517–44. https://doi.org/10.1016/j.jhg
.2009.02.002.

Ferguson, James. 1999. *Expectations of Modernity: Myths and Meanings of
Urban Life on the Zambian Copperbelt*. Berkeley: University of California
Press. https://doi.org/10.1525/9780520922280.

———. 2006. *Global Shadows: Africa in the Neoliberal World Order*. Durham:
Duke University Press. https://doi.org/10.1215/9780822387640.

Ferry, Elizabeth Emma. 2013. *Minerals, Collecting, and Value Across the
US-Mexico Border*. Bloomington: Indiana University Press.

Ferry, Elizabeth Emma, and Mandana E. Limbert. 2008. *Timely Assets: The
Politics of Resources and Their Temporalities*. 1st ed. School for Advanced
Research Advanced Seminar Series. Santa Fe: School for Advanced
Research Press.

First Nations Information Governance Centre. 2014. *Ownership, Control,
Access and Possession (OCAPTM): The Path to First Nations Information
Governance*. Ottawa: First Nations Information Governance Centre.
http://books.scholarsportal.info/en/read?id=/ebooks/ebooks4/cpdc4
/2018-12-11/3/10095457.

Fischer, Edward F. 2014. *The Good Life: Aspiration, Dignity, and the
Anthropology of Wellbeing*. Standford: Standford University Press.

Fumoleau, René. 2004. *As Long as This Land Shall Last: A History of Treaty 8
and Treaty 11, 1870–1939*. Calgary: University of Calgary Press.

Furniss, Elizabeth. 2005. "Imagining the Frontier: Comparative Perspectives from Canada and Australia." In *Dislocating the Frontier: Essaying the Mystique of the Outback*, edited by Deborah Bird Rose and Richard Davis, 23–46. Canberra: ANU Press.

Gaudry, Adam J.P. 2011. "Insurgent Research." *Wicazo Sa Review* 26, no. 1 (Spring): 113–36. https://doi.org/10.5749/wicazosareview.26.1.0113.

———. 2016. "Fantasies of Sovereignty: Deconstructing British and Canadian Claims to Ownership of the Historic North-West." *Native American and Indigenous Studies* 3 (1): 46–74. https://doi.org/10.5749/natiindistudj.3.1.0046.

Gibson, Ginger, and Jason Klinck. 2005. "Canada's Resilient North: The Impact of Mining on Aboriginal Communities." *Pimatisiwin: A Journal of Aboriginal and Indigenous Community Health* 3, no. 1 (Spring): 115–39.

Gilberthorpe, Emma, and Glenn Banks. 2012. "Development on Whose Terms?: CSR Discourse and Social Realities in Papua New Guinea's Extractive Industries Sector." *Resources Policy* 37, no. 2 (June): 185–93. https://doi.org/10.1016/j.resourpol.2011.09.005.

Gilberthorpe, Emma, and Gavin Hilson, eds. 2016. *Natural Resource Extraction and Indigenous Livelihoods: Development Challenges in an Era of Globalization*. London: Routledge. https://doi.org/10.4324/9781315597546.

Godoy, Ricardo. 1985. "Mining: Anthropological Perspectives." *Annual Review of Anthropology* 14 (October): 199–217. https://doi.org/10.1146/annurev.an.14.100185.001215.

Golub, Alex. 2014. *Leviathans at the Gold Mine: Creating Indigenous and Corporate Actors in Papua New Guinea*. Durham: Duke University Press. https://doi.org/10.2307/j.ctv11314sg.

Goode, Judith G., and Jeff Maskovsky, eds. 2002. *New Poverty Studies: The Ethnography of Power, Politics, and Impoverished People in the United States*. New York: NYU Press.

Government of Canada, Statistics Canada. 2016. "Census Profile, 2016 Census—Canada [Country] and Canada [Country]." https://www12.statcan.gc.ca/census-recensement/2016/dp-pd/prof/details/page.cfm?Lang=E&Geo1=PR&Code1=01&Geo2=PR&Code2=01&Data=Count&SearchText=01&SearchType=Begins&SearchPR=01&B1=All&Custom=&TABID=3.

Government of Northwest Territories. 2006. *Ready to Work North: Trainer's Guide*. Yellowknife: Government of Northwest Territories.

———. 2018a. "NWT Takes Home Award for Sustainable Diamond Industry." *News Releases* (blog), June 1, 2018. https://www.gov.nt.ca/en/newsroom/news/nwt-takes-home-award-sustainable-diamond-industry.

———. 2018b. "Scenes and Stories from the Diamonds Do Good Awards." Department of Industry, Tourism and Investment, June 4, 2018. https://www.iti.gov.nt.ca/en/newsroom/scenes-and-stories-diamonds-do-good-awards.

Grant, J. Andrew, and Ian Taylor. 2004. "Global Governance and Conflict Diamonds: The Kimberley Process and the Quest for Clean Gems." *The Round Table* 93, no. 375 (July): 385–401. https://doi.org/10.1080/0035853042000249979.

Grasseni, Christina. 2013. *Beyond Alternative Food Networks: Italy's Solidarity Purchase Groups*. London: Bloomsbury Academic.

Greenberg, Jessica. 2014. *After the Revolution: Youth, Democracy, and the Politics of Disappointment in Serbia*. Stanford: Stanford University Press. https://doi.org/10.1515/9780804791175.

Hall, Rebecca Jane. 2017. "Diamonds Are Forever: A Decolonizing, Feminist Approach to Diamond Mining in Yellowknife, Northwest Territories." PhD Diss., York University. https://hdl.handle.net/10315/34474.

———. 2022. *Refracted Economies: Diamond Mining and Social Reproduction in the North*. Toronto: University of Toronto Press. https://doi.org/10.3138/9781487540852.

Halushka, John. 2016. "Work Wisdom: Teaching Former Prisoners How to Negotiate Workplace Interactions and Perform a Rehabilitated Self." *Ethnography* 17, no. 1 (March): 72–91. https://doi.org/10.1177/1466138115609625.

Haney, Lynne Allison. 2010. *Offending Women: Power, Punishment, and the Regulation of Desire*. Berkeley: University of California Press. https://doi.org/10.1525/9780520945913.

Hanrahan, Maura. 2017. "Enduring Polar Explorers' Arctic Imaginaries and the Promotion of Neoliberalism and Colonialism in Modern Greenland." *Polar Geography* 40, no. 2 (April): 102–20. https://doi.org/10.1080/1088937X.2017.1303754.

Haraway, Donna J. 1997. *Modest_Witness@Second_Millennium.FemaleMan_Meets_OncoMouse: Feminism and Technoscience*. New York: Routledge.

Harrison, Faye V., ed. 1991. *Decolonizing Anthropology: Moving Further Toward an Anthropology for Liberation*. 1st ed. Arlington: American Anthropological Association.

———, ed. 1997. *Decolonizing Anthropology: Moving Further Toward an Anthropology of Liberation*. 3rd ed. Arlington: American Anthropological Association.

Hart, Matthew. 2002. *Diamond: The History of a Cold-Blooded Love Affair*. New York: Plume.

Harvey, David. 1989. *The Condition of Postmodernity: An Enquiry into the Origins of Cultural Change*. Cambridge: Wiley-Blackwell.

Harvey, Penny, and Hannah Knox. 2015. *Roads: An Anthropology of Infrastructure and Expertise*. 1st ed. Ithaca: Cornell University Press. https://doi.org/10.7591/9780801456466.

Heiman, Rachel, Carla Freeman, and Mark Liechty. 2012. *The Global Middle Classes: Theorizing Through Ethnography*. Santa Fe: SAR Press.

Heleniak, Timothy. 1999. "Migration from the Russian North During the Transition Period." *Social Protection and Labor Policy and Technical Notes*, no. 20818. The World Bank. https://ideas.repec.org/p/wbk/hdnspu/20818.html.

Heller, Monica. 1999. *Linguistic Minorities and Modernity: A Sociolinguistic Ethnography*. 1st ed. Real Language Series. London: Longman.

Heller, Monica, and Lindsay Bell. 2012. "Frontiers and Frenchness: Pride and Profit in the Production of Canada." In Duchêne and Heller 2012, 161–82.

Heller, Monica, Lindsay A. Bell, Michelle Daveluy, Mireille McLaughlin, and Hubert Noël. 2015. *Sustaining the Nation: The Making and Moving of Language and Nation*. London: Oxford University Press. https://doi.org/10.1093/acprof:oso/9780199947195.001.0001.

Helm, June, ed. 1968. *Essays on the Problem of the Tribe*. Seattle: American Ethnological Society/University of Washington Press.

Heritage Valley Capital. n.d. "About Us." LinkedIn. Accessed November 30, 2022. https://www.linkedin.com/company/heritage-valley-capital/?originalSubdomain=ca.

Hilson, Gavin. 2006. "Championing the Rhetoric? 'Corporate Social Responsibility' in Ghana's Mining Sector." *Greener Management International* 53 (Spring): 43–56.

Historical Sketch of the Origin and Work of the Hay River Mission, Great Slave Lake, N.W.T. 2012. Neuilly sur Seine, France: Ulan Press.

Hoogeveen, Dawn. 2014. "Sub-Surface Property, Free-Entry Mineral Staking and Settler Colonialism in Canada." *Antipode* 47, no. 1 (January): 121–38. https://doi.org/10.1111/anti.12095.

Howlett, Catherine, and Rebecca Lawrence. 2019. "Accumulating Minerals and Dispossessing Indigenous Australians: Native Title Recognition as Settler-Colonialism." *Antipode* 51, no. 3 (June): 818–37. https://doi.org/10.1111/anti.12516.

Hudson's Bay Company. 1866. *The Hudson Bay Company, "A Million:" Shall We Take It? Addressed to the Shareholders of the Company by One of Themselves*. CIHM/ICMH Microfiche Series, no. 37517. London: Λ.H. Baily. https://catalog.hathitrust.org/Record/100267280.

———. 2002. "Hope, John (Fl. 1863–1884); CO 2002 August." Hudson's Bay Company Archives. Accessed November 30, 2022. https://www.gov.mb.ca/chc/archives/_docs/hbca/biographical/h/hope_john-iv.pdf.

Hughes, Jason. 2005. "Bringing Emotion to Work: Emotional Intelligence, Employee Resistance and the Reinvention of Character." *Work, Employment and Society* 19, no. 3 (September): 603–25. https://doi.org/10.1177/0950017005055675.

Huseman, Jennifer, and Damien Short. 2012. "'A Slow Industrial Genocide': Tar Sands and the Indigenous Peoples of Northern Alberta." *International Journal of Human Rights* 16, no. 1 (January): 216–37. https://doi.org/10.1080/13642987.2011.649593.

Ibbitson, John. 2010. "As Stephen Harper Touches Down, Optimism Reigns in the North." *Globe and Mail*, August 23, 2010. https://www .theglobeandmail.com/amp/news/politics/as-stephen-harper-touches -down-optimism-reigns-in-the-north/article1378105/.

Irlbacher-Fox, Stephanie. 2010. *Finding Dahshaa: Self-Government, Social Suffering, and Aboriginal Policy in Canada*. Vancouver: UBC Press.

Isard, Philip. 2010. "Northern Vision: Northern Development during the Diefenbaker Era." PhD diss., University of Waterloo, UWSpace. https://hdl.handle.net/10012/5032.

Jacka, Jerry K. 2015. "Uneven Development in the Papua New Guinea Highlands: Mining, Corporate Social Responsibility, and the 'Life Market.'" *Focaal* 2015, no. 73 (December): 57–69. https://doi.org/10.3167 /fcl.2015.730105.

———. 2018. "The Anthropology of Mining: The Social and Environmental Impacts of Resource Extraction in the Mineral Age." *Annual Review of Anthropology* 47 (October): 61–77. https://doi.org/10.1146/annurev -anthro-102317-050156.

Jimmy, Elwood, Vanessa Andreotti, and Sharon Stein. 2019. *Towards Braiding*. Guelph: Musagetes Foundation.

Jorgensen, Dan. 1997. "Who and What Is a Landowner? Mythology and Marking the Ground in a Papua New Guinea Mining Project." *Anthropological Forum* 7, no. 4 (January): 599–627. https://doi.org/10.1080 /00664677.1997.9967476.

Kalant, Amelia. 2004. *National Identity and the Conflict at Oka: Native Belonging and Myths of Postcolonial Nationhood in Canada*. 1st ed. New York: Routledge. https://doi.org/10.4324/9780203503034.

K'atl'odeeche First Nation. n.d. "Welcome to K'atl'odeeche First Nation." K'atl'odeeche First Nation. Accessed November 30, 2022. http://katlodeeche .com/.

Kawashima, Ken C. 2009. *The Proletarian Gamble: Korean Workers in Interwar Japan*. Durham: Duke University Press. https://doi.org/10.1215 /9780822392293.

Keane, Webb. 2015. "Lecture 3: Varieties of Ethical Stance." In *Four Lectures on Ethics*, edited by Michael Lambek, Webb Keane, Veena Das, Didier Fassin, 127–74. London: HAU Books. https://haubooks.org/viewbook /four-lectures-on-ethics/06_ch03.

Kirsch, Stuart. 2007. "Indigenous Movements and the Risks of Counterglobalization: Tracking the Campaign Against Papua New Guinea's Ok Tedi Mine." *American Ethnologist* 34, no. 2 (May): 303–21. https://doi.org/10.1525/ae.2007.34.2.303.

———. 2010. "Sustainable Mining." *Dialectical Anthropology* 34, no. 1 (March): 87–93. https://doi.org/10.1007/s10624-009-9113-x.

———. 2014. *Mining Capitalism: The Relationship between Corporations and Their Critics*. University of California Press. https://doi.org/10.1525 /9780520957596.

Krech, Shepard. 1984. *The Subarctic Fur Trade: Native Social and Economic Adaptations.* Vancouver: UBC Press.

Kuhn, Peter, and Arthur Sweetman. 2002. "Aboriginals as Unwilling Immigrants: Contact, Assimilation and Labour Market Outcomes." *Journal of Population Economics* 15, no. 2 (May): 331–55. https://doi .org/10.1007/s001480100083.

Kulchyski, Peter Keith. 2005. *Like the Sound of a Drum: Aboriginal Cultural Politics in Denendeh and Nunavut.* Winnipeg: University of Manitoba Press.

———. 2007. *The Red Indians: An Episodic, Informal Collection of Tales from the History of Aboriginal People's Struggles in Canada.* Winnipeg: Arbeiter Ring Publishing.

Laforce, Myriam. 2010. "L'évolution des régimes miniers au Canada : l'émergence de nouvelles formes de regulation et ses implications." *Canadian Journal of Development Studies/Revue canadienne d'études du développement* 30, nos. 1–2 (January): 49–68. https://doi.org/10.1080 /02255189.2010.9669281.

Landers, Jackson. 2016. "The Foxfire Diamond Bedazzles as Smithsonian's Newest Rock Star." *Smithsonian Magazine*, November 18, 2016. https://www .smithsonianmag.com/smithsonian-institution/foxfire-diamond-bedazzles -smithsonians-newest-rock-star-180961064/.

Larkin, Brian. 2013. "The Politics and Poetics of Infrastructure." *Annual Review of Anthropology* 42 (October): 327–43. https://doi.org/10.1146 /annurev-anthro-092412-155522.

———. 2018. "Promising Forms: The Political Aesthetics of Infrastructure." In Anand, Gupta, and Appel 2018, 175–202. https://doi.org/10.1215 /9781478002031-008.

Latour, Bruno. 1993. *We Have Never Been Modern.* Translated by Catherine Porter. Cambridge: Harvard University Press.

Lea, Tess. 2008. *Bureaucrats & Bleeding Hearts: Indigenous Health in Northern Australia.* Sydney: University of New South Wales Press.

———. 2020. *Wild Policy: Indigeneity and the Unruly Logics of Intervention.* Anthropology of Policy. Stanford: Stanford University Press. https://doi .org/10.1515/9781503612679.

Lea, Tess, and Paul Pholeros. 2010. "This Is Not a Pipe: The Treacheries of Indigenous Housing." *Public Culture* 22, no. 1 (Winter): 187–209. https://doi.org/10.1215/08992363-2009-021.

Le Billon, Philippe. 2006. "Fatal Transactions: Conflict Diamonds and the (Anti)Terrorist Consumer." *Antipode* 38, no. 4 (September): 778–801. https://doi.org/10.1111/j.1467-8330.2006.00476.x.

———. 2008. "Diamond Wars? Conflict Diamonds and Geographies of Resource Wars." *Annals of the Association of American Geographers* 98, no. 2 (April): 345–72. https://doi.org/10.1080/00045600801922422.

Legrand, Jacques. 1980. *Diamonds: Myth, Magic, and Reality.* New York: Crown Publishers.

Li, Fabiana. 2009. "Documenting Accountability: Environmental Impact Assessment in a Peruvian Mining Project." *Polar: Political and Legal Anthropology Review* 32, no. 2 (November): 218–36. https://doi.org/10.1111 /j.1555-2934.2009.01042.x.

———. 2011. "Engineering Responsibility: Environmental Mitigation and the Limits of Commensuration in Chilean Mining Project." *Focaal* 2011, no. 60 (June): 61–73. https://doi.org/doi:10.3167/fcl.2011.600106.

Li, Tania Murray. 2010. "To Make Live or Let Die? Rural Dispossession and the Protection of Surplus Populations." *Antipode* 41, no. S1 (January): 66–93. https://doi.org/10.1111/j.1467-8330.2009.00717.x.

Liboiron, Max. 2021. *Pollution Is Colonialism.* Durham: Duke University Press. https://doi.org/10.2307/j.ctv1jhvnk1.

Mackey, Eva. 2016. *Unsettled Expectations: Uncertainty, Land and Settler Decolonization.* Halifax: Fernwood Publishing.

Mains, Daniel. 2012. "Blackouts and Progress: Privatization, Infrastructure, and a Developmentalist State in Jimma, Ethiopia." *Cultural Anthropology* 27, no. 1 (February): 3–27. https://doi.org/10.1111/j.1548-1360.2012.01124.x.

Marx, Karl. 1992. *Capital: A Critique of Political Economy.* Vol. 1. Translated by Ben Fowkes. London: Penguin.

Mason, John Alden. 1946. *Notes on the Indians of the Great Slave Lake Area.* New Haven: Yale University Press.

Massumi, Brian. 2002. *Parables for the Virtual: Movement, Affect, Sensation.* Durham: Duke University Press. https://doi.org/10.1215/9780822383574.

Mazzarella, William. 2010. "Affect: What Is It Good For?" In *Enchantments of Modernity: Empire, Nation, Globalization,* edited by Saurabh Dube, 291–309. London: Routledge. https://doi.org/10.4324/9781003071020.

McCarthy, Shawn. 2003. "Kakfwi Comments Stir Controversy." *Globe and Mail,* September 9, 2003. https://www.theglobeandmail.com/report -on-business/kakfwi-comments-stir-controversy/article1166155/.

McCormack, Patricia A. 2010. *Fort Chipewyan and the Shaping of Canadian History, 1788–1920s: We like to Be Free in This Country.* Vancouver: UBC Press.

McIntosh, Andrew, and Shirlee Anne Smith. 2006. "Rupert's Land." In *The Canadian Encyclopedia.* Historica Canada. Article published February 7, 2006; last edited August 18, 2022. https://www.thecanadianencyclopedia. ca/en/article/ruperts-land.

McLaughlin, Mireille. 2013. "What Makes Art Acadian?" In *Multilingualism and the Periphery,* edited by Sari Pietikainen and Helen Kelly-Holmes, 35–54. Oxford: Oxford University Press. https://doi.org/10.1093/acprof: oso/9780199945177.003.0003.

———. 2015. "Linguistic Minorities and the Multilingual Turn: Constructing Language Ownership Through Affect in Cultural Production." *Multilingua* 35 (4): 393–414. https://doi.org/10.1515/multi-2015-0008.

MITAC. 2005. *Prospecting the Future.* Ottawa: MITAC. https://www.yumpu .com/en/document/read/16405401/prospecting-the-future-mihr.

Moffitt, Morgan, Courtney Chetwynd, and Zoe Todd. 2015. "Interrupting the Northern Research Industry: Why Northern Research Should Be in Northern Hands." *Northern Public Affairs* 4 (1): 32–37.

Mogstad, Heidi, and Lee-Shan Tse. 2018. "Decolonizing Anthropology: Reflections from Cambridge." *Cambridge Journal of Anthropology* 36, no. 2 (September): 53–72. https://doi.org/10.3167/cja.2018.360206.

Moore, Henrietta L. 2011. *Still Life: Hopes, Desires and Satisfactions*. 1st ed. Cambridge: Polity.

Moreton-Robinson, Aileen. 2015. *The White Possessive: Property, Power, and Indigenous Sovereignty*. Minneapolis: University of Minnesota Press. https://doi.org/10.5749/minnesota/9780816692149.001.0001.

Muehlebach, Andrea. 2012. *The Moral Neoliberal: Welfare and Citizenship in Italy*. Chicago: University of Chicago Press.

Nash, June. 1979. *We Eat the Mines and the Mines Eat Us: Dependency and Exploitation in Bolivian Tin Mines*. New York: Columbia University Press.

———. 1981. "Ethnographic Aspects of the World Capitalist System." *Annual Review of Anthropology* 10 (October): 393–423. https://doi.org/10.1146/annurev.an.10.100181.002141.

Newhouse, David, and Evelyn Peters, eds. 2003. *Not Strangers in These Parts: Urban Aboriginal Peoples*. Ottawa: Policy Research Initiative. https://publications.gc.ca/pub?id=9.686648&sl=0.

Nugent, David. 1994. "Building the State, Making the Nation: The Bases and Limits of State Centralization in 'Modern' Peru." *American Anthropologist* 96, no. 2 (June): 333–69. https://doi.org/10.1525/aa.1994.96.2.02a00040.

O'Malley, Martin. 1976. *The Past and Future Land: An Account of the Berger Inquiry into the Mackenzie Valley Pipeline*. Toronto: P. Martin Associates.

On the Move Partnership. n.d. "On the Move Partnership." Accessed September 10, 2019. https://www.onthemovepartnership.ca/.

Orttung, Robert W. 2016. *Sustaining Russia's Arctic Cities: Resource Politics, Migration, and Climate Change*. Oxford: Berghahn Books. https://doi.org/10.1515/9781785333163.

Pahuja, Nisha, and Manfred Becker, dirs. 2007. *Diamond Road*. Documentary. Toronto: Kensington Communications.

Paine, Robert. 1990. "Advocacy and Anthropology." *American Anthropologist* 92, no. 3 (September): 742–3. https://doi.org/10.1525/aa.1990.92.3.02a00150.

Palmer, Craig T., and Peter R. Sinclair. 2000. "Expecting to Leave: Attitudes to Migration a Mong High School Students on the Great Northern Peninsula of Newfoundland." *Newfoundland Studies* 16, no. 1 (January): 30–46.

Parson, Sean, and Emily Ray. 2018. "Sustainable Colonization: Tar Sands as Resource Colonialism." *Capitalism Nature Socialism* 29, no. 3 (July): 68–86. https://doi.org/10.1080/10455752.2016.1268187.

Peck, Jamie, and Nikolas Theodore. 2000. "Beyond 'Employability.'"
    Cambridge Journal of Economics 24, no. 6 (November): 729–49. https://doi
    .org/10.1093/cje/24.6.729.
Petrov, Andrey N. 2007. "Revising the Harris-Todaro Framework to Model
    Labour Migration from the Canadian Northern Frontier." *Journal of
    Population Research* 24, no. 2 (November): 185–206. https://doi.org
    /10.1007/BF03031930.
Piper, Liza. 2009. *The Industrial Transformation of Subarctic Canada*. Vancouver:
    UBC Press.
Porter, John. 1965. *The Vertical Mosaic: An Analysis of Social Class and Power
    in Canada*. Studies in the Structure of Power: Decision-Making in Canada
    2. Toronto: University of Toronto Press. https://doi.org/10.3138
    /9781442683044.
Povinelli, Elizabeth A. 2002. *The Cunning of Recognition: Indigenous Alterities
    and the Making of Australian Multiculturalism*. Durham: Duke University
    Press. https://doi.org/10.1215/9780822383673.
———. 2008. "The Child in the Broom Closet: States of Killing and Letting
    Die." *South Atlantic Quarterly* 107, no. 3 (Summer): 509–30. https://doi
    .org/10.1215/00382876-2008-004.
Prashad, Vijay. 2000. *The Karma of Brown Folk*. Minneapolis: University
    of Minnesota Press.
Preston, Jen. 2017. "Racial Extractivism and White Settler Colonialism: An
    Examination of the Canadian Tar Sands Mega-Projects." *Cultural Studies* 31,
    nos. 2–3 (May): 353–75. https://doi.org/10.1080/09502386.2017.1303432.
Purser, Gretchen, and Brian Hennigan. 2017. "'Work as Unto the Lord':
    Enhancing Employability in an Evangelical Job-Readiness Program."
    Qualitative Sociology 40, no. 1 (March): 111–33. https://doi.org/10.1007
    /s11133-016-9347-2.
Rajak, Dinah. 2009. "I Am the Conscience of the Company': Responsibility
    and the Gift in a Transnational Mining Corporation." In *Economics and
    Morality: Anthropological Approaches*, edited by Katherine E. Browne and
    B. Lynne Milgram, 190–200. Lanham: AltaMira Press.
———. 2011. *In Good Company: An Anatomy of Corporate Social Responsibility*.
    Stanford: Stanford University Press. https://doi.org/10.1515
    /9780804781619.
Rajchman, John. 2001. *The Deleuze Connections*. Cambridge: MIT Press.
    https://doi.org/10.7551/mitpress/2323.001.0001.
Richardson, Tanya, and Gisa Weszkalnys. 2014. "Introduction: Resource
    Materialities." *Anthropology Quarterly* 87, no. 1 (Winter): 5–30. https://doi
    .org/10.1353/anq.2014.0007.
Roseberry, William. 1989. *Anthropologies and Histories: Essays in Culture,
    History, and Political Economy*. New Brunswick: Rutgers University Press.
Sahlins, Marshall. 1999. "What Is Anthropological Enlightenment? Some
    Lessons of the Twentieth Century." *Annual Review of Anthropology* 28
    (October): i–xxiii. https://doi.org/10.1146/annurev.anthro.28.1.0.

Said, Edward W. 1978. *Orientalism*. Wolfgang Laade Music of Man Archive. London: Routledge & Kegan Paul.

———. 1989. "Representing the Colonized: Anthropology's Interlocutors." *Critical Inquiry* 15, no. 2 (Winter): 205–25. https://doi.org/10.1086/448481.

Sandlos, John, and Arn Keeling. 2016. "Toxic Legacies, Slow Violence, and Environmental Injustice at Giant Mine, Northwest Territories." *The Northern Review* 42 (July): 7–21. https://doi.org/10.22584/nr42.2016.002.

Sawyer, Suzana. 2004. *Crude Chronicles: Indigenous Politics, Multinational Oil, and Neoliberalism in Ecuador*. American Encounters/Global Interactions. Durham: Duke University Press. https://doi.org/10.1215/9780822385752.

Sawyer, Suzana, and Edmund Terence Gomez, eds. 2012. *The Politics of Resource Extraction: Indigenous Peoples, Multinational Corporations, and the State*. International Political Economy Series. New York: Palgrave Macmillan; United Nations Research Institute for Social Development. https://doi.org/10.1057/9780230368798.

Sayer, Andrew. 2000. "Moral Economy and Political Economy." *Studies in Political Economy* 61, no. 1 (January): 79–103. https://doi.org/10.1080/19187033.2000.11675254.

Schiller, Nina Glick. 2012. "Unravelling the Migration and Development Web: Research and Policy Implications." In *Migration and Development Buzz? Rethinking the Migration Development Nexus and Policies*, ed. Birgitte Mossin Brønden, special issue, *International Migration* 50, no. 3 (June): 92–7. https://doi.org/10.1111/j.1468-2435.2012.00757.x.

Schwenkel, Christina. 2015. "Sense." *Fieldsights* (blog). Society for Cultural Anthropology, September 24, 2015. https://culanth.org/fieldsights/sense.

Scott, James C. 1976. *The Moral Economy of the Peasant*. New Haven: Yale University Press.

———. 1999. *Seeing Like a State*. New Haven: Yale University Press. https://yalebooks.yale.edu/book/9780300078152/seeing-state.

Scott, Jamie S. 2005. "Cultivating Christians in Colonial Canadian Missions." In *Canadian Missionaries, Indigenous Peoples: Representing Religion at Home and Abroad*, edited by Alvyn J. Austin and Jamie S. Scott, 21–45. Toronto: University of Toronto Press. https://doi.org/10.3138/9781442672253-003.

Sharp, John. 2006. "Corporate Social Responsibility and Development: An Anthropological Perspective." *Development Southern Africa* 23, no. 2 (June): 213–22. https://doi.org/10.1080/03768350600707892.

Sider, Gerald. 1987. "When Parrots Learn to Talk, and Why They Can't: Domination, Deception, and Self-Deception in Indian-White Relations." *Comparative Studies in Society and History* 29, no. 1 (January): 3–23. https://doi.org/10.1017/S0010417500014328.

———. 2003a. *Between History and Tomorrow: Making and Breaking Everyday Life in Rural Newfoundland*. Toronto: University of Toronto Press.

———. 2003b. *Living Indian Histories: Lumbee and Tuscarora People in North Carolina*. Chapel Hill: University of North Carolina Press.

———. 2006. "The Production of Race, Locality, and State: An Anthropology." *Anthropologica* 48 (2): 247–63. https://doi.org/10.2307/25605314.

Sider, Gerald, and Gavin Smith, eds. 1997. *Between History and Histories: The Making of Silences and Commemorations*. 1st ed. Toronto: University of Toronto Press. https://doi.org/10.3138/9781442671324.

Simone, AbdouMaliq. 2012. "Infrastructure: Commentary by AbdouMaliq Simone." *Cultural Anthropology*. Accessed November 30, 2022. https://journal.culanth.org/index.php/ca/infrastructure-abdoumaliq-simone.

Simpson, Audra. 2014. *Mohawk Interruptus: Political Life Across the Borders of Settler States*. Durham: Duke University Press. https://doi.org/10.1215/9780822376781.

Simpson, Leanne Betasamosake. 2021. *A Short History of the Blockade: Giant Beavers, Diplomacy, and Regeneration in Nishnaabewin*. Edmonton: University of Alberta Press.

Slowey, Gabrielle A. 2008. *Navigating Neoliberalism: Self-Determination and the Mikisew Cree First Nation*. Vancouver: UBC Press.

Smith, David M. 1992. "The Dynamics of a Dene Struggle for Self-Determination." *Anthropologica* 34 (1): 21–49. https://doi.org/10.2307/25605631.

Smith, Vicki. 2010. "Review Article: Enhancing Employability: Human, Cultural, and Social Capital in an Era of Turbulent Unpredictability." *Human Relations* 63, no. 2 (November): 279–300. https://doi.org/10.1177/0018726709353639.

Sonntag, Selma K. 2005. "Appropriating Identity or Cultivating Capital? Global English in Offshoring Service Industries." *Anthropology of Work Review* 26, no. 1 (March): 13–20. https://doi.org/10.1525/awr.2005.26.1.13.

Sosa, Irene, and Karyn Keenan. 2001. *Impact Benefit Agreements Between Aboriginal Communities and Mining Companies: Their Use in Canada*. Toronto: Canadian Environmental Law Association; Vancouver: Environmental Mining Council of British Columbia; Lima: CooperAcción.

Spitzer, Aaron. 2008. "Northwest Territories." In *Lonely Planet Canada*. 10th ed. Fort Mill: Lonely Planet.

Standing, Guy. 2011. *The Precariat: The New Dangerous Class*. London: Bloomsbury Academic.

Star, Leigh Susan. 1999. "The Ethnography of Infrastructure." *American Behavioural Scientist* 43, no. 3 (November): 377–91. https://doi.org/10.1177/00027649921955326.

Starn, Orin. 2011. "Here Come the Anthros (Again): The Strange Marriage of Anthropology and Native America." *Cultural Anthropology* 26, no. 2 (May): 179–204. https://doi.org/10.1111/j.1548-1360.2011.01094.x.

Statistics Canada. 2007. "Diamonds in the Ice." *Canada Year Book Overview 2007*, September 7, 2007. *Canada Year Book*, no. 11-402-X. https://www150.statcan.gc.ca/n1/pub/11-402-x/2007/1130/ceb1130_003-eng.htm.

Steur, Luisa. 2014. "An 'Expanded' Class Perspective: Bringing Capitalism Down to Earth in the Changing Political Lives of Adivasi Workers in Kerala." *Modern Asian Studies; Cambridge* 48, no. 5 (September): 1334–57. https://doi.org/10.1017/S0026749X14000407.

Stevenson, Lisa. 2014. *Life Beside Itself: Imagining Care in the Canadian Arctic*. Berkeley: University of California Press. https://doi.org/10.1525/9780520958555.

Stoler, Ann Laura. 2010. *Along the Archival Grain: Epistemic Anxieties and Colonial Common Sense*. Princeton: Princeton University Press. https://doi.org/10.1515/9781400835478.

Stuhl, Andrew. 2013. "The Politics of the 'New North': Putting History and Geography at Stake in Arctic Futures." *The Polar Journal* 3, no. 1 (June): 94–119. https://doi.org/10.1080/2154896X.2013.783280.

———. 2016. *Unfreezing the Arctic: Science, Colonialism, and the Transformation of Inuit Lands*. Chicago: University of Chicago Press.

Tasky, Frank. 1971. *Tapwe* [Hay River newspaper clipping].

Taussig, Michael T. 1980. *The Devil and Commodity Fetishism in South America*. Chapel Hill: University of North Carolina Press.

Todd, Zoe. 2016. "From Classroom to River's Edge: Tending to Reciprocal Duties Beyond the Academy (Commentary)." *Aboriginal Policy Studies* 6, no. 1 (October): 90–7. https://doi.org/10.5663/aps.v6i1.27448.

———. 2017. "Commentary: The Environmental Anthropology of Settler Colonialism, Part I." *Engagement: A Blog Published by the Anthropology and Environment Society* (blog). Anthropology and Environment Society, April 11, 2017. https://aesengagement.wordpress.com/2017/04/11/commentary-the-environmental-anthropology-of-settler-colonialism-part-i/.

———. 2018. "Should I Stay or Should I Go?" *Anthro{dendum}* (blog). May 12, 2018. https://anthrodendum.org/2018/05/12/should-i-stay-or-should-i-go/.

———. 2020. "(An Answer)." *Anthro{dendum}* (blog). January 27, 2020. https://anthrodendum.org/2020/01/27/an-answer/.

Trouillot, Michel-Rolph. 1995. *Silencing the Past: Power and the Production of History*. Boston: Beacon Press.

True Colors International. n.d. "About." Accessed November 30, 2022. https://www.truecolorsintl.com/about.

Tsing, Anna. 2000. "Inside the Economy of Appearances." *Public Culture* 12, no. 1 (Winter): 115–44. https://doi.org/10.1215/08992363-12-1-115.

———. 2005. *Friction: An Ethnography of Global Connection*. Princeton: Princeton University Press. https://doi.org/10.1515/9781400830596.

Tuck, Eve. 2014. "ANCSA as X-Mark: Surface and Subsurface Claims of the Alaska Native Claims Settlement Act." In *Transforming the University: Alaska Native Studies in the 21st Century: Proceedings from the Alaska Native Studies Conference 2013*, edited by Beth Ginondidoy Leonard, Jeane T'áaw xíwaa Breinig, Lenora Ac'aralek Carpluk, Sharon Chilux Lind, and Maria Shaa Tláa Williams, 240–72. Minneapolis: Two Harbors Press.

Tuck, Eve, and K. Wayne Yang. 2012. "Decolonization Is Not a Metaphor." *Decolonization: Indigeneity, Education & Society* 1, no. 1 (September): 1–40.

Urciuoli, Bonnie. 2008. "Skills and Selves in the New Workplace." *American Ethnologist* 35, no. 2 (May): 211–28. https://doi.org/10.1111/j.1548 -1425.2008.00031.x.

Veracini, Lorenzo. 2011. "Introducing, Settler Colonial Studies." *Settler Colonial Studies* 1, no. 1 (September): 1–12. https://doi.org/10.1080/2201473X .2011.10648799.

Vlassenroot, Koen, and Steven Van Bockstael, eds. 2008. *Artisanal Diamond Mining: Perspectives and Challenges*. Ghent: Academia Press.

Voloshinov, Valentin Nikolaevich. 1973. *Marxism and the Philosophy of Language*. Translated by Mikhail Mikhaïlovich Bakhtin. New York: Seminar Press.

Walsh, Andrew. 2003. "'Hot Money' and Daring Consumption in a Northern Malagasy Sapphire-Mining Town." *American Ethnologist* 30, no. 2 (May): 290–305. https://doi.org/10.1525/ae.2003.30.2.290.

———. 2010. "The Commodification of Fetishes: Telling the Difference Between Natural and Synthetic Sapphires." *American Ethnologist* 37, no. 1 (February): 98–114. https://doi.org/10.1111/j.1548-1425.2010.01244.x.

Watkins, Mel, ed. 1977. *Dene Nation: The Colony Within*. Toronto: University of Toronto Press. https://doi.org/10.3138/9781487574451.

Weber, Max. 1948. *From Max Weber: Essays in Sociology*. Translated by C. Wright Mills and Hans H. Gerth. New York: Oxford University Press.

Welker, Marina. 2009. "'Corporate Security Begins in the Community': Mining, the Corporate Responsibility Industry, and Environmental Advocacy in Indonesia." *Cultural Anthropology* 24, no. 1 (February): 142–79. https://doi.org/10.1111/j.1548-1360.2009.00029.x.

———. 2012. "The Green Revolution's Ghost: Unruly Subjects of Participatory Development in Rural Indonesia." *American Ethnologist* 39, no. 2 (May): 389–406. https://doi.org/10.1111/j.1548-1425.2012.01371.x.

———. 2014. *Enacting the Corporation: An American Mining Firm in Post-Authoritarian Indonesia*. 1st ed. Berkeley: University of California Press. https://doi.org/10.1525/9780520957954.

Welker, Marina, Damani J. Partridge, and Rebecca Hardin. 2011. "Corporate Lives: New Perspectives on the Social Life of the Corporate Form: An Introduction to Supplement 3." *Current Anthropology* 52, no. S3 (April): S3–16. https://doi.org/10.1086/657907.

West, Paige. 2012. *From Modern Production to Imagined Primitive*. Durham: Duke University Press. https://doi.org/10.1515/9780822394846.

Weszkalnys, Gisa. 2016. "A Doubtful Hope: Resource Affect in a Future Oil Economy." *Journal of the Royal Anthropological Institute* 22, no. S1 (April): 127–46. https://doi.org/10.1111/1467-9655.12397.

Whitehouse, Simon. 2022a. "Mackenzie Place Sold to 'Sophisticated Western Canadian Company.'" *NNSL Media*, January 28, 2022. https://www.nnsl.com/business/mackenzie-place-sold-to-sophisticated-western-canadian-company/.

———. 2022b. "'We've Got Work to Do,' Say Visiting Mackenzie Place Owners." *NNSL Media*, April 28, 2022. https://www.nnsl.com/business/weve-got-work-to-do-say-visiting-mackenzie-place-owners/.

Wildcat, Matthew, Mandee McDonald, Stephanie Irlbacher-Fox, and Glen Coulthard. 2014. "Learning from the Land: Indigenous Land Based Pedagogy and Decolonization." In *Indigenous Land-Based Education*, ed. Matthew Wildcat, Stephanie Irlbacher-Fox, Glen Coulthard, and Mandee McDonald, special issue, *Decolonization: Indigeneity, Education & Society* 3, no. 3 (December): iv–xv.

Williams, Raymond Henry. 1977. *Marxism and Literature*. Oxford: Oxford University Press.

Wilson, Emma, and Florian Stammler. 2016. "Beyond Extractivism and Alternative Cosmologies: Arctic Communities and Extractive Industries in Uncertain Times." *The Extractive Industries and Society* 3, no. 1 (January): 1–8. https://doi.org/10.1016/j.exis.2015.12.001.

Wolf, Eric R. 1982. *Europe and the People Without History*. Berkeley: University of California Press.

———. 1986. "The Vicissitudes of the Closed Corporate Peasant Community." *American Ethnologist* 13, no. 2 (May): 325–9. https://doi.org/10.1525/ae.1986.13.2.02a00080.

Wolfe, Patrick. 1999. *Settler Colonialism and the Transformation of Anthropology: The Politics and Poetics of an Ethnographic Event*. London: Cassell.

Woolford, Andrew. 2015. *This Benevolent Experiment: Indigenous Boarding Schools, Genocide, and Redress in Canada and the United States*. Lincoln: University of Nebraska Press.

Zarchikoff, William W. 1975. "The Development and Settlement Patterns of Hay River Northwest Territories." Unpublished MA thesis, Simon Fraser University.

Index

Note: The letter *f* following a page number denotes a figure; the letter *m*, a map.

mine, 30–1; blame and taking responsibility, 106–7; and church, 54–5; curse-or-cure dichotomy of mining, 136–7; English learning, 54; entanglement in extractive industry, 134–5, 136; in extraction of resources, 25–6, 83–4, 123–4; family names given to, 43n1; "from the communities" phrase, 104–5; and the future, 134–5, 136, 137; hunting and fishing rights, 51, 55; in IBAs and SEAs, 34–5; impact of mining and extraction, 136–7, 143–4; improvement of lives through diamond mining, 116–18; land title and claims, 51, 57–8; mobilities, 92–5, 98; quality of life assessment, 25–6; regional solidarity, 56, 57–8; registration of children, 124; research approach of author, 16–17; and settler Canadians, 7–8, 15–16, 25–6; sovereignty and rights, 130–1; and stories about diamonds, 2–3; transience in, 58; and work, 21, 35, 42, 46, 83–4. *See also* individual nations and groups; specific topics
Indigenous people (globally), impact of mining, 13n1
Indigenous people in Canada: migration research framing, 92–3; treaty system, 51; vocational schools, 53
Indigenous scholars, and anthropology in the North, 15–16
"Indigenous," terminology, 15
Indigenous women (generally): aspiration, 120, 133; education, 94; entanglement in extractive industry, 120, 123, 125, 127, 136; impact of mining, 119–20. *See also* individual women
infrastructural prospecting, 71–2, 142

infrastructure: in architectures of extraction, 64, 73, 77, 140, 143; corporate contributions to community, 129–30; description, 12; for promised development, 67–8, 143; role and meaning, 64–5, 78–9; skate park in Hay River, 127–8, 129
infrastructures (technological and social), and cultural life, 11–12
international immigration in the North, 82–6
Introduction to Underground Mining course, 97
inuksuk in Hay River, 63, 77–8
Inuvialuit people, 57
Ipili people, 14

Joanne (Hay River resident), 128, 129, 131
job readiness program in Hay River. *See* training program in diamond mining
job training, as regulation or control, 105
job training programs, description, 42

K'atl'odeeche First Nation: as community, 60; in Hay River town and area, 53–4, 56–7, 57n6, 68, 70; on map of Hay River, 41m; as reservation, 56–7, 59–60; travel to Hay River, 40, 59
Keane, Webb, 128
kimberlite, 31
Kirsch, Stuart, 137
Krogman, Naomi, 35

Lackenbauer, Whitney, 69
Lacy (Hay River resident), 131
Laforce, Myriam, 35
lamproite, 31
land negotiations, in region of proposed mines, 30

▣ TEACHING CULTURE
Ethnographies for the Classroom

Editor: John Barker, University of British Columbia

This series is an essential resource for instructors searching for ethnographic case studies that are contemporary, engaging, provocative, and created specifically with undergraduate students in mind. Written with clarity and personal warmth, books in the series introduce students to the core methods and orienting frameworks of ethnographic research and provide a compelling entry point to some of the most urgent issues faced by people around the globe today.

Recent Books in the Series

Fat in Four Cultures: A Global Ethnography of Weight by Cindi Sturtz-Sreetharan, Alexandra Brewis, Jessica Hardin, Sarah Trainer, and Amber Wutich (2021)

Esperanza Speaks: Confronting a Century of Global Change in Rural Panama by Gloria Rudolf (2021)

The Living Inca Town: Tourist Encounters in the Peruvian Andes by Karoline Guelke (2021)

Collective Care: Indigenous Motherhood, Family, and HIV/AIDS by Pamela J. Downe (2021)

I Was Never Alone, or Oporniki: An Ethnographic Play on Disability in Russia by Cassandra Hartblay (2020)

Millennial Movements: Positive Social Change in Urban Costa Rica by Karen Stocker (2020)

From Water to Wine: Becoming Middle Class in Angola by Jess Auerbach (2020)

Deeply Rooted in the Present: Heritage, Memory, and Identity in Brazilian Quilombos by Mary Lorena Kenny (2018)

Long Night at the Vepsian Museum: The Forest Folk of Northern Russia and the Struggle for Cultural Survival by Veronica Davidov (2017)

Truth and Indignation: Canada's Truth and Reconciliation Commission on Indian Residential Schools, second edition, by Ronald Niezen (2017)

Merchants in the City of Art: Work, Identity, and Change in a Florentine Neighborhood by Anne Schiller (2016)

Ancestral Lines: The Maisin of Papua New Guinea and the Fate of the Rainforest, second edition, by John Barker (2016)

Love Stories: Language, Private Love, and Public Romance in Georgia by Paul Manning (2015)

Culturing Bioscience: A Case Study in the Anthropology of Science by Udo Krautwurst (2014)